Learning Helm
Managing Apps on Kubernetes

Matt Butcher, Matt Farina, and Josh Dolitsky

Beijing · Boston · Farnham · Sebastopol · Tokyo

Learning Helm

by Matt Butcher, Matt Farina, and Josh Dolitsky

Published by O'Reilly Media, Inc., 1005 Gravenstein Highway North, Sebastopol, CA 95472.

O'Reilly books may be purchased for educational, business, or sales promotional use. Online editions are also available for most titles (*http://oreilly.com*). For more information, contact our corporate/institutional sales department: 800-998-9938 or *corporate@oreilly.com*.

Acquisitions Editor: John Devins	**Indexer:** Sue Klefstad
Development Editor: Jeff Bleiel	**Interior Designer:** David Futato
Production Editor: Christopher Faucher	**Cover Designer:** Karen Montgomery
Copyeditor: Tom Sullivan	**Illustrator:** Kate Dullea
Proofreader: Kim Cofer	

January 2021:   First Edition

Revision History for the First Edition
2021-01-20:   First Release

See *http://oreilly.com/catalog/errata.csp?isbn=9781492083658* for release details.

978-1-492-08365-8

[LSI]

Table of Contents

Preface

Helm is the package manager for Kubernetes, the popular open source container management platform.

Package managers make platforms more accessible to those who use them. In order to use a platform like Kubernetes, you need to run software on it, and much of that software will be off-the-shelf or shared. Package managers like Helm enable you to install and start using the software quickly without needing to figure out how to make it run or run well on the platform, because it has already been packaged up in an easy-to-use manner.

If you have software you want to share with others, package managers make it easy to do. Platforms are more useful when there is a wide variety of software to run on them; open source projects and companies both like to make their software easy to install on the platforms it runs on, and Helm makes this possible for Kubernetes.

Package managers aren't just for sharing and consuming others' software, however. They are often an integral part of other systems, such as DevOps tooling, and they are used as a building block.

Virtually every modern platform has a package manager. Operating systems, programming languages, and cloud platforms all have package managers of some form.

In this book you will learn about Helm, which provides modern package management for Kubernetes, and the packages, called charts, that you can use with it. You will learn how to use Helm, how to create packages, and how to share those packages with other platforms.

Who Should Read This Book

There are a few situations where you will find this book useful.

If you're new to Kubernetes or want to learn how to install off-the-shelf applications, this book will help you learn how to do that with Helm. It is much easier and faster to install applications through Helm than it is to learn how to do so by hand with Kubernetes.

If you work for a company (or a project) that wants to distribute your applications to Kubernetes users in an easy-to-consume manner, this book will teach you how to do that with Helm. Being able to quickly install your application makes getting started easier, and Helm can help you with that.

This book is also for DevOps professionals who want to learn to use Kubernetes package management as part of their DevOps toolchains. Helm provides powerful and advanced features that can be used as building blocks for other automation. These have been used to deploy large and complex applications onto Kubernetes, and this book will teach you how to leverage those features.

Why We Wrote This Book

We, the authors, are maintainers of Helm, so we set out to write a book to help those who have questions about it. We didn't just want to supply the technical details that are often found in the documentation; we wanted to provide context and insight into what Helm does and why.

Navigating This Book

The first three chapters introduce you to Helm and show you how to use the Helm client. This begins in Chapter 1 with an overview of where Helm sits within the cloud native ecosystem along with an overview of its architecture. Chapters 2 and 3 address using the Helm client, beginning with installing Helm and progressing to advanced usage.

Chapters 4 through 6 cover creating packages for Helm. This begins with how to create a package (Chapter 4), moves into learning the template syntax (Chapter 5), and finishes with advanced features (Chapter 6). If you want to create packages for Helm, these chapters are for you.

Sharing packages, including their individual release versions, is covered in Chapter 7. Sharing is important if you are distributing software to others or sharing it between systems while using DevOps processes.

Helm can be extended, which is covered in Chapter 8. There are opportunities to customize Helm without needing to fork or contribute functionality to Helm.

Two appendixes are provided with reference material. Appendix A provides an overview of differences between current and legacy packages, while Appendix B covers the repository API used for sharing packages.

Conventions Used in This Book

The following typographical conventions are used in this book:

Italic
: Indicates new terms, URLs, email addresses, filenames, and file extensions.

`Constant width`
: Used for program listings, as well as within paragraphs to refer to program elements such as variable or function names, databases, data types, environment variables, statements, and keywords.

`Constant width bold`
: Shows commands or other text that should be typed literally by the user.

`Constant width italic`
: Shows text that should be replaced with user-supplied values or by values determined by context.

This element signifies a tip or suggestion.

This element signifies a general note.

This element indicates a warning or caution.

Using Code Examples

Supplemental material (code examples, exercises, etc.) is available for download at *https://github.com/masterminds/learning-helm*.

If you have a technical question or a problem using the code examples, please send email to *bookquestions@oreilly.com*.

This book is here to help you get your job done. In general, if example code is offered with this book, you may use it in your programs and documentation. You do not need to contact us for permission unless you're reproducing a significant portion of the code. For example, writing a program that uses several chunks of code from this book does not require permission. Selling or distributing examples from O'Reilly books does require permission. Answering a question by citing this book and quoting example code does not require permission. Incorporating a significant amount of example code from this book into your product's documentation does require permission.

We appreciate, but generally do not require, attribution. An attribution usually includes the title, author, publisher, and ISBN. For example: "*Learning Helm* by Matt Butcher, Matt Farina, and Josh Dolitsky (O'Reilly). Copyright 2021 Matt Butcher, Innovating Tomorrow, and Blood Orange, 978-1-492-08365-8."

If you feel your use of code examples falls outside fair use or the permission given above, feel free to contact us at *permissions@oreilly.com*.

O'Reilly Online Learning

 For more than 40 years, *O'Reilly Media* has provided technology and business training, knowledge, and insight to help companies succeed.

Our unique network of experts and innovators share their knowledge and expertise through books, articles, and our online learning platform. O'Reilly's online learning platform gives you on-demand access to live training courses, in-depth learning paths, interactive coding environments, and a vast collection of text and video from O'Reilly and 200+ other publishers. For more information, visit *http://oreilly.com*.

How to Contact Us

Please address comments and questions concerning this book to the publisher:

O'Reilly Media, Inc.
1005 Gravenstein Highway North
Sebastopol, CA 95472
800-998-9938 (in the United States or Canada)
707-829-0515 (international or local)
707-829-0104 (fax)

We have a web page for this book, where we list errata, examples, and any additional information. You can access this page at *https://oreil.ly/learning-helm*.

Email *bookquestions@oreilly.com* to comment or ask technical questions about this book.

For news and information about our books and courses, visit *http://oreilly.com*.

Find us on Facebook: *http://facebook.com/oreilly*

Follow us on Twitter: *http://twitter.com/oreillymedia*

Watch us on YouTube: *http://youtube.com/oreillymedia*

Acknowledgments

This book has benefited from the attention of our official technical reviewers: Taylor Thomas, Jonathan Johnson, and Michael Hausenblas.

We would like to express our appreciation for everyone at O'Reilly who helped bring this project together. This is especially true of John Devins and Jeff Bleiel. The process of writing the book was delightful.

The Helm ecosystem was created by a legion of contributors from all around the globe. Individuals, nongovernmental organizations, and corporations have cooperated to build a technology that meets a broad array of needs. From building charts to contributing fixes to helping others learn Helm, individuals have devoted time and energy to improving the community and code for all. We deeply appreciate their work.

Most of all, we want to thank our wives and children for their patience and love throughout the process.

## CHAPTER 1

Introducing Helm

Helm is the package manager for Kubernetes. That is the way the Helm developers have described Helm since the very first commits to the Git repository. And that sentence is the topic of this chapter.

In this chapter, we will start with a conceptual look at the cloud native ecosystem, in which Kubernetes is a key technology. We will take a fresh look at what Kubernetes has to offer to set the stage for describing Helm.

Next, we will look at the problems Helm sets out to solve. In this section, we will look at the concept of package management and why we have modeled Helm this way. We will also visit some of the unique facets of installing packages into a cluster management tool like Kubernetes.

Finally, we will finish the chapter with a high-level look at Helm's architecture, focusing on the concepts of charts, templates, and releases. By the end of the chapter, you will understand how Helm fits into the broader ecosystem of tools, and you will be familiar with the terminology and concepts we will be using throughout this book.

The Cloud Native Ecosystem

The emergence of cloud technologies has clearly changed the way the industry looks at hardware, system management, physical networking, and so on. Virtual machines replaced physical servers, storage services displaced talk of hard drives, and automation tools rose in prominence. This was perhaps an early change in the way the industry conceptualized the cloud. But as the strengths and weaknesses of this new approach became clearer, the practices of designing applications and services also began to shift.

Developers and operators began to question the practice of building large single-binary applications that executed on beefy hardware. They recognized the difficulty of sharing data across different applications while retaining data integrity. Distributed locking, storage, and caching became mainstream problems instead of points of academic interest. Large software packages were broken down into smaller discrete executables. And, as Kubernetes founder Brendan Burns often puts it, "distributed computing went from an advanced topic to Computer Science 101."

The term *cloud native* captures this cognitive shift in what one might call our *architectural view* of the cloud. When we design our systems around the capabilities and constraints of the cloud, we are designing cloud native systems.

Containers and Microservices

At the very heart of cloud native computing is this philosophical perspective that *smaller discrete standalone services* are preferable to *large monolithic services* that do everything. Instead of writing a single large application that handles everything from generating the user interface to processing task queues to interacting with databases and caches, the cloud native approach is to write a series of smaller services, each relatively special purpose, and then join these services together to serve a higher-level purpose. In such a model, one service might be the sole user of a relational database. Services that wish to access the data will contact that service over (typically) a representational state transfer (REST) API. And, using JavaScript Object Notation (JSON) over HTTP, these other services will query and update data.

This breakdown allows developers to hide the low-level implementation and instead offer a set of features specific to the business logic of the broader application.

Microservices

Where once an application consisted of a single executable that did all of the work, cloud native applications are *distributed applications*. While separate programs each take responsibility for one or two discrete tasks, together these programs all form a single logical application.

With all this theory, a simple example may better explain how this works. Imagine an ecommerce website. We can think of several tasks that jointly comprise this sort of website. There is a product catalog, user accounts and shopping carts, a payment processor that handles the security-sensitive process of monetary transactions, and a frontend through which customers view items and select their purchases. There is also an administrative interface where the store owners manage inventory and fulfill orders.

Historically, applications like this were once built as one single program. The code responsible for each of these units of work was all compiled together into one large executable, which was then often run on a single large piece of hardware.

The cloud native approach to such an application, though, is to break this ecommerce application into multiple pieces. One handles payment transactions. Another tracks the product catalog. Yet another provides the administrative, and so on. These services then communicate with each other over the network using well-defined REST APIs.

Taken to an extreme, an application is broken down into its smallest constituent parts, and each part is a program. This is the *microservice architecture*. Standing at the opposite end of the spectrum of a monolithic application, a microservice is responsible for handling only one small part of the overall application's processing.

The microservice concept has had an outsized influence on the evolution of cloud native computing. And nowhere is this more evident than in the emergence of *container computing*.

Containers

It is common to compare and contrast a container and a virtual machine. A virtual machine runs an entire operating system in an isolated environment on a host machine. A container, in contrast, has its own filesystem, but is executed in the same operating system kernel as the host.

But there is a second way of conceptualizing the container—one that may prove more beneficial for the present discussion. As its name suggests, a *container* provides a useful way of packaging up the runtime environment for a single program so that the executable is guaranteed to have all of its dependencies satisfied when it is moved from one host to another.

This is a more philosophical approach, perhaps, because it imposes some non-technical restrictions on a container. For example, one could package a dozen different programs in a single container and execute them all at the same time. But containers, at least as they were designed by Docker, were intended as a vehicle for one top-level program.

 When we talk about programs here, we're really thinking at a higher level of abstraction than "a binary." Most Docker containers have at least a few executables that are there merely to assist the main program. But these executables are auxiliary to the primary function of the container. For example, a web server may require a few other local utilities for starting up or performing low-level tasks (Apache, for example, has tools for modules), but it is the web server itself that is the primary program.

Containers and microservices are, by design, a perfect match. Small discrete programs can be packaged, along with all their dependencies, into svelte containers. And those containers can be moved around from host to host. When executing a container, the host need not have all the tools required to execute the program because all of those tools are packaged within the container. The host merely must have the ability to run containers.

For example, if a program is built in Python 3, the host does not need to install Python, configure it, and then install all the libraries that the program requires. All of that is packaged in the container. When the host executes the container, the correct version of Python 3 and each required library is already stored in the container.

Taking this one step further, a host can freely execute containers with competing requirements. A containerized Python 2 program can run in the same host as a containerized Python 3 requirement, and the host's administrators need not do any special work to configure these competing requirements!

These examples illustrate one of the features of the cloud native ecosystem: administrators, operators, and site reliability engineers (SREs) are no longer in the business of managing program dependencies. Instead, they are free to focus on a higher level of resource allocation. Rather than fretting over which versions of Python, Ruby, and Node are running on different servers, operators can focus on whether network, storage, and CPU resources are correctly allocated for these containerized workloads.

Running a program in complete isolation is sometimes useful. But more often, we want to expose some aspects of this container to the outside world. We want to give it access to storage. We want to allow it to answer network connections. And we want to inject tidbits of configuration into the container based on our present needs. All of these tasks (and more still) are provided by the container runtime. When a container declares that it has a service that is internally listening on port 8080, the container runtime may grant it access on the host port 8000. Thus, when the host gets a network request on port 8000, the container sees this as a request on its port 8080. Likewise, a host can mount a filesystem into the container, or set specific environment variables inside of the container. In this way, a container can participate in the broader environment around it—including not just other containers on that host, but remote services on the local network or even the internet.

Container images and registries

Container technology is a sophisticated and fascinating space in its own right. But for our purposes, we only need to understand a few more things about how containers work before be can proceed to the next layer of the cloud native stack.

As we discussed in the previous section, a container is a program together with its dependencies and environment. This whole thing can be packaged together into a portable representation called a *container image* (often just referred to as an *image*).

Images are not packaged into one large binary; instead, they are packaged into discrete *layers*, each of which has its own unique identifier. When images are moved around, they are moved as a collection of layers, which provides a huge advantage. If one host has an image with five layers and another host needs the same image, it only needs to fetch the layers that it doesn't already have. So if it has two of the five layers already, it only needs to fetch three layers to rebuild the entire container.

There is a crucial piece of technology that provides the ability to move container images around. An *image registry* is a specialized piece of storage technology that houses containers, making them available for hosts. A host can *push* a container image to a registry, which transfers the layers to the registry. And then another host can *pull* the image from the registry to the host's environment, after which the host can execute the container.

The registry manages the layers. When one host requests an image, the registry lets the host know which layers compose that image. The host can then determine which layers (if any) are missing and subsequently download just those layers from the registry.

A registry uses up to three pieces of information to identify a particular image:

Name
> An image *name* can range from simple to complex, depending on the registry that stores the image: `nginx`, `servers/nginx`, or `example.com/servers/nginx`.

Tag
> The *tag* typically refers to the version of the software installed (`v1.2.3`), though tags are really just arbitrary strings. The tags `latest` and `stable` are often used to indicate "the most recent version" and "the most recent production-ready version," respectively.

Digest
> Sometimes it is important to pull a very specific version of an image. Since tags are *mutable*, there is no guarantee that at any given time a tag refers to *exactly* a specific version of the software. So registries support fetching images by *digest*, which is a SHA-256 or SHA-512 digest of the image's layer information.

Throughout this book, we will see images referenced using the three preceding pieces of information. The canonical format for combining these is `name:tag@digest`, where only `name` is required. Thus, `example.com/servers/nginx:latest` says "give me the tag `latest` for the image named `example.com/servers/nginx`." And

```
example.com/my/app@sha256:
a428de44a9059feee59237a5881c2d2cffa93757d99026156e4ea544577ab7f3
```

says "give me `example.com/my/app` with the exact digest given here."

While there is plenty more to learn about images and containers, we have enough knowledge now to move on to the next important topic: schedulers. And in that section, we'll discover Kubernetes.

Schedules and Kubernetes

In the previous section we saw how containers encapsulate individual programs and their required environment. Containers can be executed locally on workstations or remotely on servers.

As developers began packaging their applications into containers and operators began using containers as an artifact for deployment, a new set of questions emerged. How do we best execute lots of containers? How do we best facilitate a microservice architecture where lots of containers need to work together? How do we judiciously share access to things like network attached storage, load balancers, and gateways? How do we manage injecting configuration information into lots of containers? And perhaps most importantly, how do we manage resources like memory, CPU, network bandwidth, and storage space?

Moving even one level beyond, people began asking (based on their experiences with virtual machines) how one might manage distributing containers across multiple hosts, spreading the load equitably while still judiciously using resources? Or, more simply, how do we run the fewest possible hosts while running as many containers as we need?

In 2015, the time was right: Docker containers were making inroads into the enterprise. And there was a clear need for a tool that could manage container scheduling and resource management across hosts. Multiple technologies landed on the scene: Mesos introduced Marathon; Docker created Swarm; Hashicorp released Nomad; and Google created an open source sibling to its internal Borg platform, and named this technology Kubernetes (the Greek word for a ship's captain).

All of these projects were providing an implementation of a clustered container management system that could schedule containers and wire them up for hosting sophisticated microservice-like distributed applications.

Each of these schedulers had strengths and weaknesses. But Kubernetes introduced two concepts that set it apart from the crowd: *declarative infrastructure* and the *reconciliation loop*.

Declarative infrastructure

Consider the case of deploying a container. One might approach the process of deploying a container like this: I create the container. I open a port for it to listen on, and then I attach some storage at this particular place on the filesystem. Then I wait for everything to be initialized. Then I test it to see if the container is ready. Then I mark it as available.

In this approach, we are thinking *procedurally* by focusing on the process of setting up a container. But Kubernetes' design is that we think *declaratively*. We tell the scheduler (Kubernetes) what our desired state is, and Kubernetes takes care of converting that declarative statement into its own internal procedures.

Installing a container on Kubernetes, then, is more a matter of saying, "I want this container running on this port with this amount of CPU and some storage mounted at this location on the filesystem." Kubernetes works behind the scenes to wire everything up according to our declaration of what we want.

The reconciliation loop

How does Kubernetes work behind the scenes to do all of this? When we viewed things procedurally, there was a certain order of operations there. How does Kubernetes know the order? This is where the idea of the *reconciliation loop* comes into play.

In a reconciliation loop, the scheduler says "here is the user's desired state. Here is the current state. They are not the same, so I will take steps to reconcile them." The user wants storage for the container. Currently there is no storage attached. So Kubernetes creates a unit of storage and attaches it to the container. The container needs a public network address. None exists. So a new address is attached to the container. Different subsystems in Kubernetes work to fulfill their individual part of the user's overall declaration of desired state.

Eventually, Kubernetes will either succeed in creating the user's desired environment or will arrive at the conclusion that it cannot realize the user's desires. Meanwhile, the user takes a passive role in observing the Kubernetes cluster and waiting for it to achieve success or mark the installation as failed.

From containers to pods, services, deployments, etc.

While concise, the preceding example is a little misleading. Kubernetes doesn't necessarily treat the container as the unit of work. Instead, Kubernetes introduces a higher-level abstraction called a *pod*. A pod is an abstract envelope that describes a discrete unit of work. A pod describes not just a container, but one or more containers (as well as their configuration and requirements) that together perform one unit of work:

```
apiVersion: v1 ❶
kind: Pod
metadata:
    name: example-pod
spec:
    containers: ❷
```

```
    - image: "nginx:latest"
      name: example-nginx
```

❶ The first two lines define the Kubernetes kind (v1 Pod).

❷ A pod can have one or more containers.

Most frequently, a pod only has one container. But sometimes they have containers that do some preconfiguration for the main container, exiting before the main container comes online. These are called *init containers*. Other times, there are containers that run alongside the main container and provide auxiliary services. These are called *sidecar containers*. These are all considered part of the same pod.

 In the preceding code, we have written a definition of a Kubernetes Pod resource. These definitions, when expressed as YAML or JSON, are referred to as *manifests*. A manifest can contain one or more Kubernetes *resources* (also called *objects* or *resource definitions*). Each resource is associated with one of the Kubernetes *types*, such as a Pod or Deployment. In this book, we typically use *resource* because the word *object* is overloaded: YAML defines the word *object* to mean a named key/value structure.

A Pod describes what configuration the container or containers need (such as network ports or filesystem mount points). Configuration information in Kubernetes may be stored in *ConfigMaps* or, for sensitive information, *Secrets*. And the Pod's definition may then relate those ConfigMaps and Secrets to environment variables or files within each container. As Kubernetes sees those relationships, it will attempt to attach and configure the configuration data as described in the Pod definition:

```
apiVersion: v1 ❶
kind: ConfigMap
metadata:
    name: configuration-data
data: ❷
    backgroundColor: blue
    title: Learning Helm
```

❶ In this case, we have declared a v1 ConfigMap object.

❷ Inside of data, we declare some arbitrary name/value pairs.

A Secret is structurally similar to a ConfigMap, except that the values in the data section must be Base64 encoded.

Pods are linked to configuration objects (like ConfigMap or Secret) using *volumes*. In this example, we take the previous Pod example and attach the Secret above:

```
apiVersion: v1
kind: Pod
metadata:
    name: example-pod
spec:
    volumes: ❶
    - name: my-configuration
      configMap:
          name: configuration-data ❷
    containers:
    - image: "nginx:latest"
      name: example-nginx
      env: ❸
        - name: BACKGROUND_COLOR ❹
          valueFrom:
            configMapKeyRef:
                name: configuration-data ❺
                key: backgroundColor ❻
```

❶ The volumes section tells Kubernetes which storage sources this pod needs.

❷ The name configuration-data is the name of our ConfigMap we created in the previous example.

❸ The env section injects environment variables into the container.

❹ The environment variable will be named BACKGROUND_COLOR inside of the container.

❺ This is the name of the ConfigMap it will use. This map must be in volumes if we want to use it as a filesystem volume.

❻ This is the name of the key inside the data section of the ConfigMap.

A pod is the "primitive" description of a runnable unit of work, with containers as part of that pod. But Kubernetes introduces higher-order concepts.

Consider a web application. We might not want to run just one instance of this web application. If we ran just one, and it failed, our site would go down. And if we wanted to upgrade it, we would have to figure out how to do so without taking down the whole site. Thus, Kubernetes introduced the concept of a *Deployment*. A Deployment describes an application as a collection of identical pods. The Deployment is composed of some top-level configuration data as well as a template for how to construct a replica pod.

With a Deployment, we can tell Kubernetes to create our app with a single pod. Then we can scale it up to five pods. And back down to three. We can attach a *Horizontal-*

PodAutoscaler (another Kubernetes type) and configure that to scale our pod based on resource usage. And when we upgrade the application, the Deployment can employ various strategies for incrementally upgrading individual pods without taking down our entire application:

```
apiVersion: apps/v1 ❶
kind: Deployment
metadata:
    name: example-deployment
    labels:
        app: my-deployment
spec:
    replicas: 3 ❷
    selector:
        matchLabels:
            app: my-deployment
    template: ❸
        metadata:
            labels:
                app: my-deployment
        spec:
            containers:
            - image: "nginx:latest"
              name: example-nginx
```

❶ This is an apps/v1 Deployment object.

❷ Inside of the spec, we ask for three replicas of the following template.

❸ The template specifies how each replica pod should look.

When it comes to attaching a Kubernetes application to other things on the network, Kubernetes provides *Service* definitions. A Service is a persistent network resource (sort of like a static IP) that persists even if the pod or pods attached to it go away. In this way, Kubernetes Pods can come and go while the network layer can continue to route traffic to the same Service endpoint. While a Service is an abstract Kubernetes concept, behind the scenes it may be implemented as anything from a routing rule to an external load balancer:

```
apiVersion: v1 ❶
kind: Service
metadata:
  name: example-service
spec:
  selector:
    app: my-deployment ❷
  ports:
    - protocol: TCP ❸
      port: 80
      targetPort: 8080
```

❶ The kind is v1 Service.

❷ This Service will route to pods with the app: my-deployment label.

❸ TCP traffic to port 80 of this Service will be routed to port 8080 on the pods that match the app: my-deployment label.

The Service described will route traffic to the Deployment we created earlier.

We've introduced a few of the many Kubernetes types. There are dozens more that we could cover, but the most frequently used by far are Pod, Deployment, ConfigMap, Secret, and Service. In the next chapter we will begin working with these concepts more directly. But for now, armed with some generic information, we can introduce Helm.

Helm's Goals

Up to this point, we have focused on the broader cloud native ecosystem and on Kubernetes' role within that ecosystem. In this section, we will change focus to Helm.

In the previous section, we saw several distinct Kubernetes resources: A Pod, a ConfigMap, a Deployment, and a Service. Each of these performs some discrete role. But an *application* typically requires more than one of these.

For example, the WordPress CMS system can be run inside of Kubernetes. But typically it would need at least a Deployment (for the WordPress server), a ConfigMap for configuration and probably a Secret (to keep passwords), a few Service objects, a StatefulSet running a database, and a few role-based access control (RBAC) rules. Already, a Kubernetes description of a basic WordPress site would span thousands of lines of YAML. At the very core of Helm is this idea that all of those objects can be packaged to be installed, updated, and deleted *together*.

When we wrote Helm, we had three main goals:

1. Make it easy to go from "zero to Kubernetes"
2. Provide a package management system like operating systems have
3. Emphasize security and configurability for deploying applications to Kubernetes

We will look at each of these three goals, and then take a look at one other aspect of Helm's usage: its participation in the life cycle management story.

From Zero to Kubernetes

The Helm project started in 2015, a few months before the inaugural KubeCon. Kubernetes was difficult to set up, often requiring new users to compile the Kubernetes source code and then use some shell scripts to get Kubernetes running. And once the cluster was up, new users were expected to write YAML (as we did in previous sections) from scratch. There were few basic examples and no production-ready examples.

We wanted to invert the learning cycle: instead of requiring users to start with basic examples and try to construct their own applications, we wanted to provide users with ready-made production-ready examples. Users could install those examples, see them in action, and then learn how Kubernetes worked.

That was, and still is to this day, our first priority with Helm: make it easier to get going with Kubernetes. In our view, a new Helm user with an existing Kubernetes cluster should be able to go from download to an installed application in five minutes or less.

But Helm isn't *just* a learning tool. It is a package manager.

Package Management

Kubernetes is like an operating system. At its foundation, an operating system provides an environment for executing programs. It provides the tools necessary to store, execute, and monitor the life cycle of a program.

Instead of executing programs, it executes containers. But similar to an operating system, it provides the tools necessary to store, execute, and monitor those containers.

Most operating systems are supported by a *package manager*. The job of the package manager is to make it easy to find, install, upgrade, and delete the programs on an operating system. Package managers provide semantics for bundling programs into installable applications, and they provide a scheme for storing and retrieving packages, as well as installing and managing them.

As we envisioned Kubernetes as an operating system, we quickly saw the need for a Kubernetes package manager. From the first commit to the Helm source code repository, we have consistently applied the package management metaphor to Helm:

- Helm provides package repositories and search capabilities to find what Kubernetes applications are available.
- Helm has the familiar install, upgrade, and delete commands.
- Helm defines a method for configuring packages prior to installing them.

- Additionally, Helm has tools for seeing what is already installed and how it is configured.

We initially modeled Helm after Homebrew (a package manager for macOS) and Apt (the package manager for Debian). But as Helm has matured, we have sought to learn from as many different package managers as we can.

There are some differences between typical operating systems and Kubernetes. One of them is that Kubernetes supports running many instances of the same application. While I may only install the database MariaDB once on my workstation, a Kubernetes cluster could be running tens, hundreds, or even thousands of MariaDB installations—each with a different configuration or even a different version.

Another notion that is rare in typical operating systems, but is central to Kubernetes, is the idea of a *namespace*. In Kubernetes, a namespace is an arbitrary grouping mechanism that defines a boundary between the things inside the namespace and the things outside. There are many different ways to organize resources with namespaces, but oftentimes they are used as a fixture to which security is attached. For example, perhaps only specific users can access resources inside of a namespace.

These are just a few ways that Kubernetes differs from traditional operating systems. These and other differences have presented challenges in the design of Helm. We have had to build Helm to take advantage of these differences, but without giving up on our package management metaphor.

For example, the Helm installation command requires not only the name of the package, but also a user-supplied name by which the installed version of that package will be referenced. In the next chapter, we'll see examples of this.

Likewise, operations in Helm are namespace-sensitive. One can install the same application into two different namespaces, and Helm provides tools to manage these different instances of the application.

In the end, though, Helm remains firmly in the package management class of tools.

Security, Reusability, and Configurability

Our third goal with Helm was to focus on three "must haves" for managing applications in a cluster:

1. Security
2. Reusability
3. Configurability

In short, we wanted to make Helm aware enough about these principles that Helm users can have confidence in the packages they use. A user should be able to *verify* that a package came from a trustworthy source (and was not tampered with), *reuse* the same package multiple times, and *configure* the package to fit their needs.

Whereas Helm's developers have direct control over the previous two design goals, this one is unique: Helm can only provide the right tools for *package authors* and hope that these creators choose to realize these three "must haves."

Security

Security is a broad category. In this context, though, we are referring to the idea that when a user examines a package, the user has the ability to verify certain things about the package:

- The package comes from a trusted source.
- The network connection over which the package is pulled is secured.
- The package has not been tampered with.
- The package can be easily inspected so the user can see what it does.
- The user can see what configuration the package has, and see how different inputs impact the output of a package.

Throughout this book, and especially in Chapter 6, we will cover security in more detail. But these five capabilities are things we believe we have provided with Helm.

Helm provides a *provenance* feature to establish verification about a package's origin, author, and integrity. Helm supports Secure Sockets Layer/Transport Layer Security (SSL/TLS) for securely sending data across the network. And Helm provides dry-run, template, and linting commands to examine packages and their possible permutations.

Reusability

A virtue of package management is its ability to install the same thing repeatedly and predictably. With Helm, this idea is extended slightly: we may want to even install the same thing (repeatedly and predictably) into the same cluster or even same namespace in a cluster.

Helm charts are the key to reusability. A chart provides a pattern for producing the same Kubernetes manifests. But charts also allow users to provide additional configuration (which we will talk about in the next chapter). So Helm provides patterns for storing configuration so that the combination of a chart plus its configuration can even be done repeatedly.

In this way, Helm encourages Kubernetes users to package their YAML into charts so that these descriptions can be reused.

In the Linux world, each Linux distribution has its own package manager and repositories. This is not the case in the Kubernetes world. Helm was constructed so that all Kubernetes distributions could share the same package manager, and (with very, very few exceptions) the same packages as well. When there are differences between two different Kubernetes distributions, charts can accommodate this using templates (discussed more thoroughly in Chapter 5) coupled with configuration.

Configurability

Helm provides patterns for taking a Helm chart and then supplying some additional configuration. For example, I might install a website with Helm, but want to set (at installation time) the name of that website. Helm provides tools to configure packages at installation time, and to reconfigure installations during upgrades. But a word of caution is in order.

Helm is a package manager. Another class of software handles *configuration management*. This class of software, typified by Puppet, Ansible, and Chef, focuses on how a given piece of software (often packaged) is *specifically configured* for its host environment. Its responsibility is to manage configuration changes over time.

Helm was not designed to be a configuration management tool, though there is at least some overlap between package management and configuration management.

Package management is typically confined to implementing three verbs: install, upgrade, and delete. Configuration management is a higher-order concept that focuses on managing an application or applications over time. This is sometimes called "day-two ops."

While Helm did not set out to be a configuration management tool, it is sometimes used as one. Organizations rely upon Helm not just to install, upgrade, and delete, but also to track changes over time, to track configuration, and to determine whether an application as a whole is running. Helm can be stretched this way, but if you want a strong configuration management solution, you may want to leverage other tools in the Helm ecosystem. Many tools like Helmfile, Flux, and Reckoner have filled in details in the larger configuration management story.

 The Helm community has created a wealth of tools that interoperate with or augment Helm. The Helm project maintains a list of those tools in the official documentation (*https://oreil.ly/hOqca*).

One of the common themes you will notice in Helm charts is that configuration options are often set up so that you can take the same chart and release a minimal version of it into your development environment, or (with different configuration options) a sophisticated version into your production environment.

Helm's Architecture

In the final section of this chapter, we will briefly turn to the high-level architecture of Helm. As well as rounding out the conceptual discussion of cloud native Kubernetes applications and package management, this section paves the way for Chapter 2, where we will dive into using Helm.

Kubernetes Resources

We have had a look at several kinds of Kubernetes resources. We saw a couple of `Pod` definitions, a `ConfigMap`, a `Deployment`, and a `Service`. There are dozens more provided by Kubernetes. You can even use custom resource definitions (CRDs) for defining your own custom resource types. The main Kubernetes documentation provides both accessible guides and detailed API documentation on each kind.

Throughout this book, we will use many different Kubernetes resource types. While we discuss them in context, you may find it beneficial to skim through the main Kubernetes document as you run across new resource definitions.

As we discussed earlier, resource definitions are *declarative*. You, the user, describe for Kubernetes the desired state of a resource. For example, you can read the `Pod` definition we created earlier in the chapter as a statement that, "I want Kubernetes to make me a `Pod` that has these features." It is up to Kubernetes to figure out how to configure and run a pod according to your specification.

All Kubernetes resource definitions share a common subset of elements. The following manifest uses a `Deployment` to illustrate the main structural elements of a resource definition:

```
apiVersion: apps/v1 ❶
kind: Deployment ❷
metadata: ❸
    name: example-deployment ❹
    labels: ❺
        some-name: some-value
    annotations: ❻
        some-name: some-value
# resource-specific YAML
```

❶ The API family and version for this resource.

❷ The kind of resource. Combined with `apiVersion`, we get the "resource type".

❸ The `metadata` section contains top-level data about the resource.

❹ A `name` is required for almost every resource type.

❺ Labels are used to give Kubernetes query-able "handles" to your resources.

❻ Annotations provide a way for authors to attach their own keys and values to a resource.

Of particular note, a *resource type* in Kubernetes is composed of three pieces of information:

API group (or family)
  Several base resource types like Pod and ConfigMap omit this name.

API version
  Expressed as a v, followed by a major version and an optional stability marker. For example, v1 is a stable "version 1," while v1alpha indicates an unstable "version 1 alpha 1."

Resource kind
  The (capitalized) name of the specific resource within the API group.

While a full resource type name is something like apps/v1 Deployment or v1 Pod (for core types), Kubernetes users will often omit the group and version when talking or writing about well-known types. For example, in this book we simply write Deployment instead of apps/v1 Deployment. Fully qualified names are used when specifying an exact version or when discussing a resource type defined in a CRD.

Thus, apps/v1 Deployment indicates that the API group "apps" has a "version 1" (stable) resource kind called "Deployment."

Kubernetes supports two main formats for declaring the resources you want: JSON and YAML. Strictly speaking, YAML is a *superset* of JSON. All JSON documents are valid YAML, but YAML adds a number of additional features.

In this book, we stick to the YAML format. We find it easier to read and write, and almost all Helm users choose YAML over JSON. However, should your preferences differ, both Kubernetes and Helm support plain JSON.

Earlier, we introduced the term *manifest*. A manifest is just a Kubernetes resource serialized to either its JSON or YAML format. It would be fair to call our earlier Pod, ConfigMap, Deployment, and Service examples each a *Kubernetes manifest*, since they are resources expressed in YAML.

Charts

We have already talked about Helm packages in this chapter. In Helm's vocabulary, a package is called a *chart*. The name is a play on the nautical nature of Kubernetes (which means "ship's captain" in Greek) and Helm (which is the steering mechanism of a ship). A chart plots the way a Kubernetes application should be installed.

A chart is a set of files and directories that adhere to the chart specification for describing the resources to be installed into Kubernetes. Chapter 4 explains the chart structure in detail, but there are a few high-level concepts we will introduce here.

A chart contains a file called *Chart.yaml* that describes the chart. It has information about the chart version, the name and description of the chart, and who authored the chart.

A chart contains *templates* as well. These are Kubernetes manifests (like we saw earlier in this chapter) that are potentially annotated with templating directives. We will cover these in detail in Chapter 5.

A chart may also contain a *values.yaml* file that provides default configuration. This file contains parameters that you can override during installation and upgrade.

These are the basic things you will find in a Helm chart, though there are others that we will cover in Chapter 4. When you see a Helm chart, though, it may be presented in either unpacked or packed form.

An *unpacked* Helm chart is just a directory. Inside, it will have a *Chart.yaml*, a *values.yaml*, a *templates/* directory, and perhaps other things as well. A *packed* Helm chart contains the same information as an unpacked one, but it is tarred and gzipped into a single file.

An unpacked chart is represented by a directory with the name of the chart. For example, the chart named *mychart* will be unpacked into a directory named *mychart/*. In contrast, a packed chart has the name *and version* of the chart, as well as the `tgz` suffix: `mychart-1.2.3.tgz`.

Charts are stored in *chart repositories*, which we will cover in Chapter 7. Helm knows how to download and install charts from repositories.

Resources, Installations, and Releases

To tie together the terminology introduced in this section, when a Helm chart is installed into Kubernetes, this is what happens:

1. Helm reads the chart (downloading if necessary).

2. It sends the values into the templates, generating Kubernetes manifests.

3. The manifests are sent to Kubernetes.

---

4. Kubernetes creates the requested resources inside of the cluster.

When a Helm chart is installed, Helm will generate as many resource definitions as it needs. Some may create one or two, others may create hundreds. When Kubernetes receives these definitions, it will create resources for them.

A Helm chart may have many resource definitions. Kubernetes sees each of these as a discrete thing. But in Helm's view all of the resources defined by a chart are related. For example, my WordPress application may have a `Deployment`, a `ConfigMap`, a `Service`, and so on. But they are all part of one *chart*. And when I install them, they are all part of the same *installation*. The same chart can be installed more than once (with a different name each time). Thus, I may have multiple installations of the same chart, just as I might have multiple resources of the same Kubernetes resource type.

And this brings us to one final term. Once we install our WordPress chart, we have an installation of that chart. Then we upgrade that chart using `helm upgrade`. Now, that installation has two releases. A new *release* of an installation is created each time we use Helm to modify the installation.

A release is created when we install a new version of WordPress. But a release is also created when we merely change the configuration of an installation, or when we roll-back an installation. This is an important feature of Helm that we will see again in Chapter 7.

A Brief Note About Helm 2

Those familiar with Helm 2 may notice certain concepts missing from this book. There is no mention of Tiller or gRPC. These things were removed from Helm 3, which is the subject of the present book. Also, this version of the book focuses on version 2 Helm charts. As confusing as it is, the Helm chart version increments separately from the Helm version. So Helm v2 used Helm Charts v1, and Helm v3 uses Helm Charts v2. These differ in a few important ways from version 1 Helm Charts—most notably in the way dependencies are declared. Helm 2 and Helm Charts v1 are considered deprecated.

Conclusion

The material here should prepare you for the coming chapters. But we hope it also provided insight into why we built Helm the way we did. Helm is only successful if it makes Kubernetes more usable both for the first-time users and for the long-time operations teams and SREs that use Helm day to day. The remainder of this book is dedicated to explaining (with lots of examples) how to get the most out of Helm—and how to do so securely and idiomatically.

## CHAPTER 2

Using Helm

Helm provides a command-line tool, named helm, that makes available all the features necessary for working with Helm charts. In this chapter, we will discover the primary features of the helm client. Along the way, we'll learn how Helm interacts with Kubernetes.

We will start by looking at how to install and configure Helm, and work our way through the main command groups in Helm. Then we will cover finding and learning about packages, and how to install, upgrade, and delete them.

Installing and Configuring the Helm Client

Helm provides a single command-line client that is capable of performing all of the main Helm tasks. This client is, appropriately enough, named helm. While there are many other tools that can work with Helm charts, this one is the official general-purpose tool maintained by the Helm core maintainers, and it is the subject of this chapter as well as the next.

The helm client is written in a programming language called Go. Unlike Python, Java-Script, or Ruby, Go is a compiled language. Once a Go program is compiled, you do not need any of the Go tools to run or otherwise work with the binary.

So we will first cover downloading and installing the static binary, and then we will briefly introduce the process for fetching and compiling from the Go source code, should you so desire.

Installing a Prebuilt Binary

Each time the Helm maintainers issue a new release of helm, the project provides new signed binary builds of helm for a number of common operating systems and architectures. At the time of this writing, prebuilt versions of Helm are available for Linux, Windows, and macOS on architectures ranging from 64-bit Intel/AMD to ARM, to s390 and PPC. This means you can run Helm on anything from a Raspberry Pi to a supercomputer.

The definitive list of Helm releases is at the Helm release page (*https://oreil.ly/L_My5*). The release page will show a chronological list of releases, with the latest release at the top.

Install with a Package Manager

Many operating system package managers, including Homebrew for macOS, Snap for Linux, and Chocolatey for Windows, can install Helm for you. We are big package management fans. Package managers make it easy to install, update, and delete your software, so we encourage you let your operating system package manager install Helm for you. But it is often wise to check whether the version in your package manager of choice is the same version that is currently marked stable on the Helm site.

A note on Helm version numbers

Until November 2020, two different major versions of Helm were actively maintained. The current stable major version of Helm is version 3. When you visit the Helm download pages, you may see both versions available for download. Because the versions are chronologically listed, it is even possible that a Helm 2 release will be newer than the latest Helm 3 release. You should use Helm 3.

Helm follows a versioning convention known as Semantic Versioning (*https://semver.org*) (SemVer). In Semantic Versioning, the version number conveys meaning about what you can expect in the release. Because Helm follows this specification, users can expect certain things out of releases simply by carefully reading the version number.

At its core, a semantic version has three numerical components and an optional *stability marker* (for alphas, betas, and release candidates). Here are some examples:

- `v1.0.0`
- `v3.3.2`
- `v2.4.22-alpha.2`

Let's talk about the numerical components first.

We often generalize this format to talk about X.Y.Z, where X is a *major version*, Y is a *minor version* and Z is a *patch release*:

- The major release number tends to be incremented infrequently. It indicates that major changes have been made to Helm, and that some of those changes may break compatibility with previous versions. The difference between Helm 2 and Helm 3 is substantial, and there is work necessary to migrate between the versions.

- The minor release number indicates feature additions. The difference between 3.2.0 and 3.3.0 might be that a few small new features were added. However, there are no *breaking changes* between versions. (With one caveat: a security fix might necessitate a breaking change, but we announce boldly when that is the case.)

- The patch release number indicates that *only* backward compatible bug fixes have been made between this release and the last one. It is always recommended to stay at the latest patch release.

When you see a release with a stability marker, like `alpha.1`, `beta.4`, or `rc.2`, appended to the release number, that means the release is considered to be a pre-release, and is not ready for mainstream production usage. In particular, Helm frequently issues *release candidates* before a major or minor update. These give the community a chance to give us some feedback on stability, compatibility, and new features before we issue a final release.

With this in mind, we are ready to proceed with the actual installation.

Downloading the binary

The easiest way to install Helm from the repository is to simply go to the releases page (*https://oreil.ly/L_My5*) and download the latest Helm 3 version.

On Windows, the download file is a ZIP archive containing a *README.md* text file, a *LICENSE* text file, and *helm.exe*.

On macOS and Linux, the download will be in a gzipped tar archive (`.tar.gz`) that can be extracted with the `tar -zxf` command. Like the Windows version, it will contain a *README.md* text file, a *LICENSE* text file, and the `helm` binary. If you are using Windows Subsystem for Linux (WSL), you should install the Linux AMD64 version into your WSL instance.

Regardless of which operating system you use, the binary is the only file you need to run Helm, and you can put it wherever you prefer on your system. It should be pre-marked as an executable, but on rare occasions in UNIX-like environments, you may also need to run the command `chmod helm +x` to set Helm to be an executable.

When installing with package managers like Homebrew (macOS), Snap (Linux), or Chocolatey (Windows), `helm` will be installed in a standard location and be made immediately available to you via the command line.

Once you have `helm` installed, you should be able to run the command `helm help` and see the Helm help text.

Using the get script to install

On macOS and Linux, you may prefer to run a shell script that will determine which version of Helm to install and do it automatically for you.

The usual sequence of commands for installing this way is as follows:

```
$ curl -fsSL -o get_helm.sh \
https://raw.githubusercontent.com/helm/helm/master/scripts/get-helm-3
$ chmod 700 get_helm.sh
$ ./get_helm.sh
```

The preceding commands fetch the latest version of the `get_helm.sh` script, and then use that to find and install the latest version of Helm 3.

For systems that automatically install Helm, such as continuous integration (CI) systems, we recommend using this method if it is important to always have the latest Helm version.

Guidance on Building from Source

Unless you are already familiar with Go development, building Helm from source can be a daunting task. You will need a version of the `make` command. Because `Makefile`-style build scripts do not follow a single standard, not all versions of `make` will work to build Helm. Gnu Make, the one most frequently used on Linux and Mac, is the one most Helm core developers use, so it is a safe bet. You will also need the `gcc` compiler and the entire Go toolchain.

In addition to these, Helm needs several auxilliary tools. Fortunately, when you run `make` the first time, it will attempt to install any additional tools that are missing.

While they are not strictly necessary, you will probably also want the `git` tool and the `kubectl` command. The `git` tool will allow you to work directly with the Helm source code repository instead of downloading source code bundles. `kubectl`, of course, is for interacting with your Kubernetes cluster. While that's not necessary for *building* Helm, it's certainly necessary when checking to see whether Helm is doing what you want it to do.

Once you have the tools installed and configured, you can simply change directories in the folder that contains Helm's source code (the directory with the *README.md* and Makefile files) and run `make build`. The first time you run this command, it will take at least several minutes. The build system must fetch lots of dependencies, including much of the Kubernetes source code, and compile it all.

 Compiling Helm for the first time can be daunting, especially if you are new to the Go programming language. Kubernetes is a sophisticated platform, and thus the Helm source code is large and difficult to build. Plan on spending at least an hour or two to get a fresh environment prepared to install Helm.

To verify that Helm is functioning correctly (especially if you have modified the source code), you can run `make test`. This will build the code, run a variety of checkers and linters, and then run the unit tests for Helm. If you plan on contributing any changes to Helm, this command *must* pass before Helm's core maintainers will even look at your requested change.

When Helm is compiled, it will be located alongside the source code in a subdirectory called *bin/*. It will not automatically be added to your executable path, so to execute the version you just built, you may need to specify the relative or exact path (e.g., *./bin/helm* or *$GOPATH/src/helm.sh/helm/bin/helm*).

If the command `helm version` correctly executes, you can be assured that you correctly compiled Helm.

From here, you can follow the detailed Developer Guide (*https://oreil.ly/X9-Ii*) to learn more. As always, if you run into problems, the `helm-users` channel on the Kubernetes Slack server is a great place to ask for help.

Working with Kubernetes Clusters

Helm interacts directly with the Kubernetes API server. For that reason, Helm needs to be able to connect to a Kubernetes cluster. Helm attempts to do this automatically by reading the same configuration files used by `kubectl` (the main Kubernetes command-line client).

Helm will try to find this information by reading the environment variable *$KUBECONFIG*. If that is not set, it will look in the same default locations that `kubectl` looks in (for example, *$HOME/.kube/config* on UNIX, Linux, and macOS).

You can also override these settings with environment variables (`HELM_KUBECONTEXT`) and command-line flags (`--kube-context`). You can see a list of environment variables and flags by running `helm help`.

The Helm maintainers recommend using kubectl to manage your Kubernetes credentials and letting Helm merely autodetect these settings. If you have not yet installed kubectl, the best place to start is with the official Kubernetes installation documentation (*https://oreil.ly/pHZIh*).

Getting Started with Helm

Whether you built Helm from source or installed using one of the aforementioned methods, at this point you should have the helm command available on your system. From here on, we will assume that Helm can be executed with the command helm (as opposed to a full or relative path, as discussed in the previous section).

In what follows, we are going to take a look at the most common workflow for starting out with Helm:

1. Add a chart repository.
2. Find a chart to install.
3. Install a Helm chart.
4. See the list of what is installed.
5. Upgrade your installation.
6. Delete the installation.

Then, in the next chapter we will dive into some of the additional features of Helm and in so doing learn more about how Helm works.

Adding a Chart Repository

Chart repositories are a topic in their own right, and in Chapter 7 we will examine them in detail. But anyone using Helm must know a few basics about chart repositories.

A Helm chart is an *individual package* that can be installed into your Kubernetes cluster. During chart development, you will often just work with a chart that is stored on your local filesystem.

But when it comes to sharing charts, Helm describes a standard format for indexing and sharing information about Helm charts. A Helm *chart repository* is simply a set of files, reachable over the network, that conforms to the Helm specification for indexing packages.

Helm 3 introduced an experimental feature for storing Helm charts in a different kind of repository: Open Container Initiative (OCI) registries (sometimes called Docker registries). In this backend, a Helm chart can be stored alongside Docker images. While this feature is not yet broadly supported, it may become the future of Helm package storage. This is discussed more in Chapter 7.

There are many—perhaps thousands of—chart repositories on the internet. The easiest way to find the popular repositories is to use your web browser to navigate to the Artifact Hub (*https://artifacthub.io*). There you will find thousands of Helm charts, each hosted on an appropriate repository.

To get started, we will install the popular Drupal content management system (*https://www.drupal.org*). This makes a good example chart because it exercises many of Kubernetes' types, including `Deployments`, `Services`, `Ingress`, and `ConfigMaps`.

Helm 2 came with a Helm repository installed by default. The `stable` chart repository was at one time the official source of production-ready Helm charts. But we realized that centralizing the charts into one repository was overly taxing to a small group of maintainers and frustrating for chart contributors.

In Helm 3, there is no default repository. Users are encouraged to use the Artifact Hub to find what they are looking for and then add their preferred repositories.

Drupal's Helm chart is located in one of the most well-curated chart repositories available: Bitnami's official Helm charts. You can take a look at the Artifact Hub's entry for the Drupal chart (*https://oreil.ly/baxxf*) for more information.

A handful of Bitnami developers were among the core contributors who designed the Helm repository system. They have contributed to the establishment of Helm's best practices for chart development and have written many of the most widely used charts.

Adding a Helm chart is done with the `helm repo add` command. Several Helm repository commands are grouped under the `helm repo` command group:

```
$ helm repo add bitnami https://charts.bitnami.com/bitnami
"bitnami" has been added to your repositories
```

The `helm repo add` command will add a repository named `bitnami` that points to the URL *https://charts.bitnami.com/bitnami*.

Now we can verify that the Bitnami repository exists by running a second `repo` command:

```
$ helm repo list
NAME    URL
bitnami https://charts.bitnami.com/bitnami
```

This command shows us all of the repositories installed for Helm. Right now, we see only the Bitnami repository that we just added.

Once we have added a repository, its index will be locally cached until we next update it (see Chapter 7). And one important thing that we can now do is search the repository.

Searching a Chart Repository

Although we know, having looked at the Artifact Hub, that the Drupal chart exists in this repository, it is still useful to search for it from the command line. Oftentimes, searching is a useful way to find not only what charts can be installed, but what versions are available.

To begin, let's search for the Drupal chart:

```
$ helm search repo drupal
NAME           CHART VERSION   APP VERSION   DESCRIPTION
bitnami/drupal 7.0.0           9.0.0         One of the most versatile open...
```

We did a simple search for the term *drupal*. Helm will search not just the package names, but also other fields like labels and descriptions. Thus, we could search for *content* and see Drupal listed there because it is a content management system:

```
$ helm search repo content
NAME                    CHART VERSION   APP VERSION   DESCRIPTION
bitnami/drupal          7.0.0           9.0.0         One of the most versa...
bitnami/harbor          6.0.1           2.0.0         Harbor is an an open...
bitnami/joomla          7.1.18          3.9.19        PHP content managemen...
bitnami/mongodb         7.14.6          4.2.8         NoSQL document-orient...
bitnami/mongodb-sharded 1.4.2           4.2.8         NoSQL document-orient...
```

While Drupal is the first result, note that there are a variety of other charts that contain the word *content* somewhere in the descriptive text.

By default, Helm tries to install the latest stable release of a chart, but you can override this behavior and install a specific verison of a chart. Thus it is often useful to see not just the summary info for a chart, but exactly which versions exist for a chart:

```
$ helm search repo drupal --versions
NAME           CHART VERSION   APP VERSION   DESCRIPTION
bitnami/drupal 7.0.0           9.0.0         One of the most versatile op...
bitnami/drupal 6.2.22          8.9.0         One of the most versatile op...
bitnami/drupal 6.2.21          8.8.6         One of the most versatile op...
bitnami/drupal 6.2.20          8.8.5         One of the most versatile op...
bitnami/drupal 6.2.19          8.8.5         One of the most versatile op...
...
```

There are several dozen versions of the Drupal chart. The preceding example has been truncated to just show the top few versions.

Chart and App Versions

A *chart version* is the version of the Helm chart. The *app version* is the version of the application packaged in the chart. Helm uses the chart version to make versioning decisions, such as which package is newest. As we can see in the preceding example, multiple chart versions may contain the same app version.

Installing a Package

In the next chapter, we will dive deeply into the details of how package installation works in Helm. In this section, though, we will look at the basic mechanics of installing a Helm chart.

At very minimum, installing a chart in Helm requires just two pieces of information: the name of the installation and the chart you want to install.

Recall that in the previous chapter we distinguished between an *installation* and a *chart*. This is an important distinction during installation and upgrading. In an operating system package manager, we may request that it install a piece of software. But it is extremely rare that we need to install the same exact package multiple times on an operating system. A Kubernetes cluster is different. It makes complete sense in Kubernetes to say "I want to install a MySQL database for Application A, and a second MySQL database for Application B." Even if the two databases are exactly the same version and have the same configuration, in order to appropriately manage our applications, we may desire to have two instances running.

Therefore, Helm needs a way to distinguish between the different instances of the same chart. So an *installation* of a chart is a specific instance of the chart. One chart may have many installations. When we run the `helm install` command, we need to give it an installation name as well as the chart name. So the most basic installation command looks something like this:

```
$ helm install mysite bitnami/drupal
NAME: mysite
LAST DEPLOYED: Sun Jun 14 14:46:51 2020
NAMESPACE: default
STATUS: deployed
REVISION: 1
NOTES:
*****************************************************************
*** PLEASE BE PATIENT: Drupal may take a few minutes to install ***
*****************************************************************
```

```
1. Get the Drupal URL:

   You should be able to access your new Drupal installation through

   http://drupal.local/

2. Login with the following credentials

   echo Username: user
   echo Password: $(kubectl get secret --namespace default mysite-drupal...
```

The preceding will create an instance of the `bitnami/drupal` chart, and will name this instance `mysite`.

As the install command runs, it will return a considerable amount of information, including user-facing instructions about getting started with Drupal.

 In future examples of `helm install`, we will omit the returned output for the sake of brevity. However, when using Helm, you will see that output for each installation. In the next chapter, we will also see how to view that output again with the `helm get` command.

At this point, there is now an instance named `mysite` in the cluster. If we tried to rerun the preceding command, we wouldn't get a second instance. Instead, we would get an error because the name `mysite` has already been used:

```
$ helm install mysite bitnami/drupal
Error: cannot re-use a name that is still in use
```

One further clarification is in order. In Helm 2, instance names were cluster-wide. You could only have an instance named `mysite` once *per cluster*. In Helm 3, naming has been changed. Now instance names are scoped to Kubernetes namespaces. We could install two instances named `mysite` as long as they each lived in a different namespace.

For example, the following is perfectly legal in Helm 3, though it would have generated a fatal error in Helm 2:

```
$ kubectl create ns first
$ kubectl create ns second
$ helm install --namespace first mysite bitnami/drupal
$ helm install --namespace second mysite bitnami/drupal
```

This will install one Drupal site named `mysite` in the `first` namespace, and an identically configured instance named `mysite` in the `second` namespace. This might seem confusing at first, but it becomes clearer when we think about a namespace as a *prefix on a name*. In that sense, we have a site named "first mysite" and another named "second mysite."

Using Namespace Flags Throughout Helm

When working with namespaces and Helm, you can use the `--namespace` or `-n` flags to specify the namespace you desire.

Configuration at Installation Time

In the preceding examples, we installed the same chart a few different ways. In all cases, they are identically configured. While the default configuration is good sometimes, more often we want to pass our own configuration to the chart.

Many charts will allow you to provide configuration values. If we take a look at the Artifact Hub page for Drupal (*https://oreil.ly/baxxf*), we would see a long list of configurable parameters. For example, we can configure the username of the Drupal admin account by setting the `drupalUsername` value.

In the next chapter we will learn how to get this information using the `helm` command.

There are several ways of telling Helm which values you want to be configured. The best way is to create a YAML file with all of the configuration overrides. For example, we can create a file that sets values for `drupalUsername` and `drupalEmail`:

```
drupalUsername: admin
drupalEmail: admin@example.com
```

Now we have a file (conventionally named *values.yaml*) that has all of our configuration. Since it is in a file, it is easy to reproduce the same installation. You can also check this file into a version control system to track changes to your values over time. The Helm core maintainers consider it a good practice to keep your configuration values in a YAML file. It is important to keep in mind, though, that if a configuration file has sensitive information (like a password or authentication token), you should take steps to ensure that this information is not leaked.

Both `helm install` and `helm upgrade` provide a `--values` flag that points to a YAML file with value overrides:

```
$ helm install mysite bitnami/drupal --values values.yaml
NAME: mysite
LAST DEPLOYED: Sun Jun 14 14:56:15 2020
NAMESPACE: default
STATUS: deployed
REVISION: 1
NOTES:
```

```
*******************************************************************
*** PLEASE BE PATIENT: Drupal may take a few minutes to install ***
*******************************************************************

1. Get the Drupal URL:

   You should be able to access your new Drupal installation through

   http://drupal.local/

2. Login with the following credentials

   echo Username: admin
   echo Password: $(kubectl get secret --namespace default mysite-drupal -o js...
```

Notice that in the preceding output the Username is now admin instead of user. One nice feature of Helm is that even the help text can be updated using values you provide.

You can specify the --values flag multiple times. Some people use this feature to have "common" overrides in one file and specific overrides in another.

There is a second flag that can be used to add individual parameters to an install or upgrade. The --set flag takes one or more values directly. They do not need to be stored in a YAML file:

```
$ helm install mysite bitnami/drupal --set drupalUsername=admin
```

This sets just one parameter, drupalUsername. This flag uses a simple key=value format.

Configuration parameters can be structured. That is, a configuration file may have multiple sections. The Drupal chart, for example, has configuration specific to the MariaDB database. These parameters are all grouped into a mariadb section. Building on our previous example, we could override the MariaDB database name like this:

```
drupalUsername: admin
drupalEmail: admin@example.com
mariadb:
  db:
    name: "my-database"
```

Subsections are a little more complicated when using the --set flag. You will need to use a dotted notation: --set mariadb.db.name=my-database. This can get verbose when setting multiple values.

In general, Helm core maintainers suggest storing configuration in *values.yaml* files (note that the filename does not need to be "values"), only using `--set` when absolutely necessary. This way, you have easy access to the values you used during an operation (and can track those over time), while also keeping your Helm commands short. Working with files also means you do not have to escape as many characters as you do when setting things on the command line.

Before moving on to upgrades, though, we will take a quick look at one of the most helpful Helm commands.

Listing Your Installations

As we have seen so far, Helm can install many things into the same cluster—even multiple instances of the same chart. And with multiple users on your cluster, different people may be installing things into the same namespace on a cluster.

The `helm list` command is a simple tool to help you see installations and learn about those installations:

```
$ helm list
NAME     NAMESPACE  REVISION  UPDATED       STATUS    CHART         APP VERSION
mysite   default    1         2020-06-14... deployed  drupal-7.0.0  9.0.0
```

This command will provide you with lots of useful information, including the name and namespace of the release, the current revision number (discussed in Chapter 1, and in more depth in the next section), the last time it was updated, the installation status, and the versions of the chart and app.

Like other commands, `helm list` is namespace aware. By default, Helm uses the namespace your Kubernetes configuration file sets as the default. Usually this is the namespace named `default`. Earlier, we installed a Drupal instance into the namespace `first`. We can see that with `helm list --namespace first`.

When listing all of your releases, one useful flag is the `--all-namespaces` flag, which will query all of the Kubernetes namespaces to which you have permission, and return all of the releases it finds:

```
$ helm list --all-namespaces
NAME     NAMESPACE  REVISION  UPDATED       STATUS    CHART         APP VERSION
mysite   default    1         2020-06-14... deployed  drupal-7.0.0  9.0.0
mysite   first      1         2020-06-14... deployed  drupal-7.0.0  9.0.0
mysite   second     1         2020-06-14... deployed  drupal-7.0.0  9.0.0
```

Upgrading an Installation

When we talk about upgrading in Helm, we talk about upgrading an installation, not a chart. An *installation* is a particular instance of a chart in your cluster. When you run `helm install`, it creates the installation. To modify that installation, use `helm upgrade`.

This is an important distinction to make in the present context because upgrading an installation can consist of two different kinds of changes:

- You can upgrade the *version of the chart*
- You can upgrade the *configuration* of the installation

The two are not mutually exclusive; you can do both at the same time. But this does introduce one new term that Helm users refer to when talking about their systems: a *release* is a particular combination of configuration and chart version for an installation.

When we first install a chart, we create the initial release of an installation. Let's call this release 1. When we perform an upgrade, we are creating a new *release* of the same *installation*: release 2. When we upgrade again, we will create release 3. (In the next chapter, we'll see how rollbacks also create releases.)

During an upgrade, then, we can create a release with new configuration, with a new chart version, or with both.

For example, say we install the Drupal chart with the `ingress` turned off. (This will effectively prevent traffic from being routed from outside the cluster into the Drupal instance.)

Note that we are using the `--set` flag to keep examples compact, but would recommend using a *values.yaml* file in regular scenarios:

```
$ helm install mysite bitnami/drupal --set ingress.enabled=false
```

With `ingress` turned off, we can work on getting our site all set up to our liking. Then when we are ready, we can create a new release that enables the `ingress` feature:

```
$ helm upgrade mysite bitnami/drupal --set ingress.enabled=true
```

In this case, we are running an `upgrade` that will only change the configuration.

In the background, Helm will load the chart, generate all of the Kubernetes objects in that chart, and then see how those differ from the version of the chart that is already installed. It will only send Kubernetes the things that need to change. In other words, Helm will attempt to alter only the bare minimum.

The preceding example will only change the `ingress` configuration. Nothing changes with the database, or even with the web server running Drupal. For that reason, nothing will be restarted or deleted and re-created. This can occasionally confuse new Helm users, but it is by design. The Kubernetes philosophy is to make changes in the most streamlined way possible, and Helm seeks to follow this philosophy.

On occasion, you may want to force one of your services to restart. This is not something you need to use Helm for. You can simply use kubectl itself to restart things. With an operating system's package manager, you do not use the package manager to restart a program. Likewise, you don't need to use Helm to restart your web server or database.

When a new version of a chart comes out, you may want to upgrade your existing installation to use the new chart version. For the most part, Helm tries to make this easy:

```
$ helm repo update ❶
Hang tight while we grab the latest from your chart repositories...
...Successfully got an update from the "bitnami" chart repository
Update Complete. ❈ Happy Helming! ❈

$ helm upgrade mysite bitnami/drupal ❷
```

❶ Fetch the latest packages from chart repositories.

❷ Upgrade the mysite release to use the latest version of bitnami/drupal.

As you can see, the default policy of Helm is to attempt to use the latest version of a chart. If you would prefer to stay on a particular version of a chart, you can explicitly declare this:

```
$ helm upgrade mysite bitnami/drupal --version 6.2.22
```

In this case, even if a newer version is released, only bitnaim/drupal version 6.2.22 will be installed.

Configuration Values and Upgrades

One of the most important things to learn about Helm installs and upgrades is that configuration gets applied freshly on each release. Here's a quick illustration:

```
$ helm install mysite bitnami/drupal --values values.yaml ❶
$ helm upgrade mysite bitnami/drupal ❷
```

❶ Install using a configuration file.

❷ Upgrade without a configuration file.

What is the result of this pair of operations? The installation will use all of the configuration data supplied in *values.yaml*, but the upgrade will not. As a result, some settings could be changed back to their defaults. This is usually not what you want.

Inspecting Values

In the next chapter we will look at the `helm get` command. You can use `helm get values mysite` to see what values were used on the last `helm install` or `helm upgrade` operation.

Helm core maintainers suggest that you provide consistent configuration with each installation and upgrade. To apply the same configuration to both releases, supply the values on each operation:

```
$ helm install mysite bitnami/drupal --values values.yaml ❶
$ helm upgrade mysite bitnami/drupal --values values.yaml ❷
```

❶ Install using a configuration file.

❷ Upgrade using the same configuration file.

One of the reasons we suggest storing configuration in a *values.yaml* file is so that this pattern is easy to reproduce. Imagine how much more cumbersome these commands would be if you used `--set` to set three or four configuration parameters! For each release, you'd have to remember exactly which things to set.

While we strongly advise using the pattern discussed here, and specifying `--values` each time, there is an upgrade shortcut available that will just reuse the last set of values that you sent:

```
$ helm upgrade mysite bitnami/drupal --reuse-values
```

The `--reuse-values` flag will tell Helm to reload the server-side copy of the last set of values, and then use those to generate the upgrade. This method is okay if you are always *just* reusing the same values. However, the Helm maintainers strongly suggest not trying to mix `--reuse-values` with additional `--set` or `--values` options. Doing so can make troubleshooting complicated and can quickly lead to unmaintainable installations in which nobody is sure how certain configuration parameters were set. While Helm does retain some state information, it is not a configuration management tool. Users are advised to manage configuration using their own tools and explicitly pass that configuration to Helm in each invocation.

At this point, we've learned how to install, list, and upgrade installations. In the final section of this chapter, we will delete an installation.

Uninstalling an Installation

To remove a Helm installation, use the `helm uninstall` command:

```
$ helm uninstall mysite
```

Note that this command does not need a chart name (`bitnami/drupal`) or any configuration files. It simply needs the name of the installation. In this section, we will look at how deletion works and take a brief detour into a big change between Helm 2 and Helm 3.

Like `install`, `list`, and `upgrade`, you can supply a `--namespace` flag to specify that you want to delete an installation *from a specific namespace*:

```
$ helm uninstall mysite --namespace first
```

The preceding will delete the site we created in the `first` namespace earlier in this chapter. Note that there is no command to delete multiple applications. You must uninstall a *specific* installation.

Deletion can take time. Larger applications may take several minutes, or even longer, as Kubernetes cleans up all of the resources. During this time, you will not be able to reinstall using the same name.

How Helm Stores Release Information

One of the big changes in Helm 3 is how it deletes Helm's own data about an installation. This section briefly describes how installations are tracked and then concludes by explaining how and why Helm changed between version 2 and version 3.

When we first install a chart with Helm (such as with `helm install mysite bitnami/drupal`), we create the Drupal application instance, and we also create a special record that contains release information. By default, Helm stores these records as Kubernetes `Secrets` (though there are other supported storage backends).

We can see these records with `kubectl get secret`:

```
$ kubectl get secret
NAME                            TYPE                                   DATA  AGE
default-token-vjhx2             kubernetes.io/service-account-token    3     58m
mysite-drupal                   Opaque                                 1     13m
mysite-mariadb                  Opaque                                 2     13m
sh.helm.release.v1.mysite.v1    helm.sh/release.v1                     1     13m
sh.helm.release.v1.mysite.v2    helm.sh/release.v1                     1     13m
sh.helm.release.v1.mysite.v3    helm.sh/release.v1                     1     7m53s
sh.helm.release.v1.mysite.v4    helm.sh/release.v1                     1     5m30s
```

We can see multiple release records at the bottom, one for each revision. As you can see, we have created four revisions of `mysite` by running `install` and `upgrade` operations.

In the next chapter, we will see how these extended records can be used to roll back to previous revisions of an installation. But we point this out now to illustrate something about how `helm uninstall` works.

When we run the command `helm uninstall mysite`, it will load the latest release record for the `mysite` installation. From that record, it will assemble a list of objects that it should remove from Kubernetes. Then Helm will delete all of those things before returning and deleting the four release records:

```
$ helm uninstall mysite
release "mysite" uninstalled
```

The `helm list` command will no longer show `mysite`:

```
$ helm list
NAME     NAMESPACE      REVISION      UPDATED STATUS   CHART     APP VERSION
```

We now have no installations. And if we rerun the `kubectl get secrets` command, we will also see all records of `mysite` have been purged:

```
$ kubectl get secrets
NAME                     TYPE                                  DATA    AGE
default-token-vjhx2      kubernetes.io/service-account-token   3       65m
```

As we can see from this output, not only were the two `Secrets` created by the Drupal chart deleted, but the four release records were deleted as well.

In the next chapter, we will see the `helm rollback` command. The preceding explanation should give you some hints as to why, by default, you cannot roll back an uninstall. It is possible, though, to delete the application, but keep the release records:

```
$ helm uninstall --keep-history
```

In Helm 2, history was retained by default. In Helm 3, the default was changed to deleting history. Different organizations prefer different policies, but core maintainers found that when most people uninstalled, they expected all traces of the installation to be destroyed.

Conclusion

In this chapter, we covered the basics of installing and then using Helm. After looking at popular methods of getting Helm installed and configured, we added a chart repository and learned how to search for charts. Then we installed, listed, upgraded, and finally uninstalled the `bitnami/drupal` chart.

Along the way, we picked up some important concepts. We learned about installations and releases. We took a first look at chart repositories, which will be covered at length in Chapter 7. And at the end of the chapter we learned a little about how Helm stores information about our installations.

In the next chapter, we will return to the `helm` command, learning about other things that the Helm tool can do.

## CHAPTER 3

Beyond the Basics with Helm

In the previous chapter, we looked at the most frequently used Helm commands. In this chapter we will explore other capabilities that the Helm tool provides. We will dive into commands that provide information about releases, that test installations, and that keep track of history. Finally, we will revisit installing and upgrading, this time covering advanced cases.

We will get started with some tools helpful for troubleshooting and debugging.

Templating and Dry Runs

When Helm installs a release, the program steps through several phases. It loads the chart, parses the values passed to the program, reads the chart metadata, and so on. Near the middle of the process, Helm compiles all of the templates in the chart (all in one pass), and then renders them by passing in the values (like we saw in the previous chapter). During this middle portion, it executes all of the template directives. Once the templates are rendered into YAML, Helm verifies the structure of the YAML by parsing it into Kubernetes objects. Finally, Helm serializes those objects and sends them to the Kubernetes API server.

Roughly, then, the process is:

1. Load the entire chart, including its dependencies.
2. Parse the values.
3. Execute the templates, generating YAML.
4. Parse the YAML into Kubernetes objects to verify the data.
5. Send it to Kubernetes.

For example, let's look at one of the commands we issued in the previous chapter:

```
$ helm install mysite bitnami/drupal --set drupalUsername=admin
```

In the first phase, Helm will locate the chart named `bitnami/drupal` and load that chart. If the chart is local, it will be read off of disk. If a URL is given, it will be fetched from the remote location (possibly using a plugin to assist in fetching the chart).

Then it will transform `--set drupalUsername=admin` into a value that can be injected into the templates. This value will be combined with the default values in the chart's *values.yaml* file. Helm does some basic checks against the data. If it has trouble parsing the user input, or if the default values are corrupt, it will exit with an error. Otherwise, it will build a single big values object that the template engine can use for substitutions.

The generated values object is created by loading all of the values of the chart file, overlaying any values loaded from files (that is, with the `-f` flag), and then overlaying any values set with the `--set` flag. In other words, `--set` values override settings from passed-in values files, which in turn override anything in the chart's default *values.yaml* file.

At this point, Helm will read all of the templates in the Drupal chart, and then execute those templates, passing the merged values into the template engine. Malformed templates will cause errors. But there are a variety of other situations that may cause failure here. For example, if a required value is missing, it is at this phase that an error is returned.

It is important to note that, when executed, some Helm templates require information about Kubernetes. So during template rendering, Helm *may* contact the Kubernetes API server. This is an important topic that we will discuss in a moment.

The output of the preceding step is then parsed from YAML into Kubernetes objects. Helm will perform some schema-level validation at this point, making sure that the objects are well-formed. Then they will be serialized into the final YAML format for Kubernetes.

In the last phase, Helm sends the YAML data to the Kubernetes API server. This is the server that `kubectl` and other Kubernetes tools interact with.

The API server will run a series of checks on the submitted YAML. If Kubernetes accepts the YAML data, Helm will consider the deployment a success. But if Kubernetes rejects the YAML, Helm will exit with an error.

Later on, we'll go into detail about what happens once the objects are sent to Kubernetes. In particular, we'll cover how Helm associates the process described earlier with an installation and revisions. But right now, we have enough information about workflow to understand two related Helm features: the `--dry-run` flag and the `helm template` command.

The --dry-run Flag

Commands like `helm install` and `helm upgrade` provide a flag named `--dry-run`. When you supply this flag, it will cause Helm to step through the first four phases (load the chart, determine the values, render the templates, format to YAML). But when the fourth phase is finished, Helm will dump a trove of information to standard output, including all of the rendered templates. Then it will exit without sending the objects to Kubernetes and without creating any release records.

For example, here is a version of our previous Drupal install with the `--dry-run` flag appended:

```
$ helm install mysite bitnami/drupal --values values.yaml --set \
drupalEmail=foo@example.com --dry-run
```

At the top of the output, it will print some information about the release:

```
NAME: mysite
LAST DEPLOYED: Tue Aug 11 11:42:05 2020
NAMESPACE: default
STATUS: pending-install
REVISION: 1
HOOKS:
```

The preceding tells us what the name of the installation is, when it was last deployed (in this case, the current date and time), which namespace it would have been deployed into, what phase of the release it is in (`pending-install`), and the revision number. Since this is an install, the revision is 1. On upgrade, it would be 2 or greater.

Finally, if this chart declared any hooks, they would be enumerated here. For more on hooks, see Chapters 6 and 7.

At first glance, it might seem that this metadata entry has a lot of unnecessary data. After all, what good does `LAST DEPLOYED` do if we are not actually installing? In fact, this chunk of information is a standard set used throughout Helm. It is part of the *release record*: a set of information about a release. Commands like `helm get` use these same fields.

Next, after the informational block, all of the rendered templates are dumped to standard output:

```
# Source: drupal/charts/mariadb/templates/test-runner.yaml
apiVersion: v1
kind: Pod
metadata:
  name: "mysite-mariadb-test-afv3u"
  annotations:
```

```
    "helm.sh/hook": test-success
spec:
  initContainers:
    - name: "test-framework"
      image: docker.io/dduportal/bats:0.4.0
...
```

The rendered Drupal chart is thousands of lines, so the preceding just shows the first several lines of output.

Finally, at the bottom of the dry-run output, Helm prints the user-oriented release notes:

```
NOTES:
********************************************************************
*** PLEASE BE PATIENT: Drupal may take a few minutes to install ***
********************************************************************

1. Get the Drupal URL:

   You should be able to access your new Drupal installation through

   http://drupal.local/
...
```

The example is truncated for brevity.

This dry-run feature provides Helm users a way to debug the output of a chart before it is sent on to Kubernetes. With all of the templates rendered, you can inspect exactly what would have been submitted to your cluster. And with the release data, you can verify that the release would have been created as you expected.

The principal purpose of the --dry-run flag is to give people a chance to inspect and debug output before sending it on to Kubernetes. But soon after it was introduced, Helm maintainers noticed a trend among users. People wanted to use --dry-run to use Helm as a template engine, and then use other tools (like kubectl) to send the rendered output to Kubernetes.

But --dry-run wasn't written with this use case in mind, and that caused a few problems:

1. --dry-run mixes non-YAML information with the rendered templates. This means the data has to be cleaned up before being sent to tools like kubectl.

2. A --dry-run on upgrade can produce different YAML output than a --dry-run on install, and this can be confusing.

3. It contacts the Kubernetes API server for validation, which means Helm has to have Kubernetes credentials even if it is just used to --dry-run a release.

---

4. It also inserts information into the template engine that is cluster-specific. Because of this, the output of some rendering processes may be cluster-specific.

To remedy these problems, the Helm maintainers introduced a completely separate command: `helm template`.

The helm template Command

While `--dry-run` is designed for debugging, `helm template` is designed to isolate the template rendering process of Helm from the installation or upgrade logic.

Earlier, we looked at the five phases of a Helm install or upgrade. The `template` command performs the first four phases (load the chart, determine the values, render the templates, format to YAML). But it does this with a few additional caveats:

- During `helm template`, Helm *never* contacts a remote Kubernetes server.
- The `template` command always acts like an installation.
- Template functions and directives that would normally require contacting a Kubernetes server will instead only return default data.
- The chart only has access to default Kubernetes kinds.

Regarding the last item, `helm template` makes a notable simplifying assumption. Kubernetes servers support built-in kinds (`Pod`, `Service`, `ConfigMap`, and so on) as well as custom kinds generated by custom resource definitions (CRDs). When running an install or upgrade, Helm fetches those kinds from the Kubernetes server before processing the chart.

However, `helm template` does this step differently. When Helm is compiled, it is compiled against a particular version of Kubernetes. The Kubernetes libraries contain the list of built-in kinds for that release. Helm uses that built-in list instead of a list it fetches from the API server. For this reason, Helm does not have access to any CRDs during a `helm template` run, since CRDs are installed on the cluster and are not included in the Kubernetes libraries.

Running an old version of Helm against a chart that uses new kinds or versions can produce an error during `helm template` because Helm will not have the newest kinds or versions compiled into it.

As a result of these decisions, `helm template` produces consistent output run after run. More importantly, it can be run in an environment that does not have access to a Kubernetes cluster, like a continuous integration (CI) pipeline.

The output is also different from --dry-run. Here's an example command:

```
$ helm template mysite bitnami/drupal --values values.yaml --set \
drupalEmail=foo@example.com
---
# Source: drupal/charts/mariadb/templates/secrets.yaml
apiVersion: v1
kind: Secret
metadata:
  name: mysite-mariadb
  labels:
    app: "mariadb"
    chart: "mariadb-7.5.1"
    release: "mysite"
    heritage: "Helm"
type: Opaque
# ... LOTS removed from here
  volumes:
    - name: tests
      configMap:
        name: mysite-mariadb-tests
    - name: tools
      emptyDir: {}
  restartPolicy: Never
```

The preceding is a greatly abridged version of the output, showing just the command and a sample of the beginning data and the end of the data. The important thing to note, though, is that *only* the YAML-formatted Kubernetes manifest is printed by default.

Because Helm does not contact a Kubernetes cluster during a helm template run, it does not do complete validation of the output. It is possible that Helm will not catch some errors in this case. You may choose to use the --validate flag if you want that behavior, but in this case Helm will need a valid *kubeconfig* file with credentials for a cluster.

The helm template command has a broad number of flags that mirror those in helm install. So in many cases, you can execute a helm template command just as you would a helm install, but then capture the YAML and use it with other tooling.

Using a Post-Render Instead of Helm Template

Sometimes you want to intercept the YAML, modify it with your own tool, and then load it into Kubernetes. Helm provides a way to execute this external tool without having to resort to using helm template. The flag --post-renderer on the install, upgrade, rollback, and template will cause Helm to send the YAML data to the command, and then read the results back into Helm. This is a great way to work with tools like Kustomize.

To summarize, `helm template` is a tool for rendering Helm charts into YAML, and the `--dry-run` flag is a tool for debugging installation and upgrade commands without loading the data into Kubernetes.

Learning About a Release

In the previous chapter, we got a glimpse of the `helm get` command. At this point, we will take a deeper look into that command and others that provide us with information *about* Helm releases.

To start, let's revisit the five phases of a Helm installation from the previous section. They were:

1. Load the chart.
2. Parse the values.
3. Execute the templates.
4. Render the YAML.
5. Send it to Kubernetes.

The first four phases are primarily concerned with a local representation of the data. That is, Helm is doing all of the processing on the same computer that the `helm` command is run on.

During the last phase, though, Helm sends that data to Kubernetes. And then the two communicate back and forth until the release is either accepted or rejected.

During that fifth phase, Helm must monitor the state of the release. Moreover, since many individuals may be working on the same copy of that particular application installation, Helm needs to monitor the state in such a way that *multiple users* can see that information.

Helm provides this feature with *release records*.

Release Records

When we install a Helm chart (with `helm install`), the new installation is created in the namespace you specify, or the default namespace. We looked at this in the previous chapter.

At the end of that chapter, we also saw how `helm install` creates a special type of Kubernetes `Secret` that holds release information. We saw how we could inspect these `Secrets` with `kubectl`:

```
$ kubectl get secret
NAME                           TYPE                                   DATA   AGE
default-token-g777k            kubernetes.io/service-account-token    3      6m
mysite-drupal                  Opaque                                 1      2m20s
mysite-mariadb                 Opaque                                 2      2m20s
sh.helm.release.v1.mysite.v1   helm.sh/release.v1                     1      2m20s
```

Of particular note is that last Secret, sh.helm.release.v1.mysite.v1. Notice that it
uses a special type (helm.sh/release.v1) to indicate that it is a Helm secret. Helm
automatically generated this secret to track version 1 of our mysite installation
(which is a Drupal site).

Each time we upgrade that mysite installation, a new Secret will be created to track
each release. In other words, a release record tracks each *revision* of an *installation*:

```
$ helm upgrade mysite bitnami/drupal
# Output omitted
$ helm upgrade mysite bitnami/drupal
# Output omitted
$ kubectl get secrets
NAME                           TYPE                                   DATA   AGE
default-token-g777k            kubernetes.io/service-account-token    3      8m43s
mysite-drupal                  Opaque                                 1      5m3s
mysite-mariadb                 Opaque                                 2      5m3s
sh.helm.release.v1.mysite.v1   helm.sh/release.v1                     1      5m3s
sh.helm.release.v1.mysite.v2   helm.sh/release.v1                     1      20s
sh.helm.release.v1.mysite.v3   helm.sh/release.v1                     1      8s
```

In the preceding example, we have upgraded a few times, and now we are at v3 of
mysite. By default, Helm tracks up to ten revisions of each installation. Once an
installation exceeds ten releases, Helm deletes the oldest release records until no more
than the maximum remain.

Each release record contains enough information to re-create the Kubernetes objects
for that revision (an important thing for helm rollback). It also contains metadata
about the release.

For example, if we looked at the release using kubectl, we would see something like
this:

```
apiVersion: v1
data:
  release: SDRzSUFFBQU... # Lots of Base64-encoded data removed
kind: Secret
metadata:
  creationTimestamp: "2020-08-11T18:37:26Z"
  labels: ❶
    modifiedAt: "1597171046"
    name: mysite
    owner: helm
    status: deployed
```

```
    version: "3"
  name: sh.helm.release.v1.mysite.v3
  namespace: default
  resourceVersion: "1991"
  selfLink: /api/v1/namespaces/default/secrets/sh.helm.release.v1.mysite.v3
  uid: cbb8b457-e331-467b-aa78-1e20360b5be6
type: helm.sh/release.v1
```

❶ The labels contain Helm metadata

In this example, the giant Base64-encoded data has been removed along with a few other inessential fields. That blob contains a gzipped representation of the chart and release. But importantly, the labels section of the Kubernetes metadata contains information about this release.

We can see, for instance, that this data describes the release named mysite, that its current revision number is 3, and the release is marked deployed. If we were to look at version 2, we would see the release status is superseded, which means that it has been replaced by a later version.

In short, this secret is stored inside of Kubernetes so that different users of the same cluster have access to the same release information.

During the life cycle of a release, it can pass through several different statuses. Here they are, approximately in the order you would likely see them:

pending-install
: Before sending the manifests to Kubernetes, Helm claims the installation by creating a release (marked version 1) whose status is set to pending-install.

deployed
: As soon as Kubernetes accepts the manifest from Helm, Helm updates the release record, marking it as deployed.

pending-upgrade
: When a Helm upgrade is begun, a new release is created for an installation (e.g., v2), and its status is set to pending-upgrade.

superseded
: When an upgrade is run, the last deployed release is updated, marked as super seded, and the newly upgraded release is changed from pending-upgrade to deployed.

pending-rollback
: If a rollback is created, a new release (e.g., v3) is created, and its status is set to pending-rollback until Kubernetes accepts the release manifest. Then it is marked deployed and the last release is marked superseded.

uninstalling

When a `helm uninstall` is executed, the most recent release is read and then its status is changed to `uninstalling`.

uninstalled

If history is preserved during deletion, then when the `helm uninstall` is complete, the last release's status is changed to `uninstalled`.

failed

Finally, if during *any* operation, Kubernetes rejects a manifest submitted by Helm, Helm will mark that release `failed`.

Listing Releases

Status messages show up in a number of Helm commands. We already saw how `pending-install` appears in a `--dry-run`. In this section and the next, we'll see a few more places where this appears.

In the previous chapter, we used `helm list` to see the charts we had installed. Given our coverage of status, it is worth revisiting `helm list`. The `list` command is the best tool for quickly checking on the statuses of your releases.

For example, say we have a cluster with both the `drupal` and `wordpress` charts installed. Here is the output of `helm list`:

```
NAME      NAMESPACE REVISION  UPDATED       STATUS    CHART            APP V...
mysite    default   3         2020-08-11... deployed  drupal-7.0.0        9.0.0
wordpress default   2         2020-08-12... deployed  wordpress-9.3.11  5.4.2
```

To show the result of a failure, though, we can run an upgrade command that we know will break:

```
$ helm upgrade wordpress bitnami/wordpress --set image.pullPolicy=NoSuchPolicy
Error: UPGRADE FAILED: cannot patch "wordpress" with kind Deployment:
Deployment.apps "wordpress" is invalid:
spec.template.spec.containers[0].imagePullPolicy: Unsupported value:
"NoSuchPolicy": supported values: "Always", "IfNotPresent", "Never"
```

As the error message indicates, a pull policy cannot be set to `NoSuchPolicy`. This error came from the Kubernetes API server, which means Helm submitted the manifest, and Kubernetes rejected it. So our release should be in a failed state.

We can verify this by running `helm ls` again:

```
$ helm ls
NAME      NAMESPACE REVISION  UPDATED     STATUS    CHART            APP VER...
mysite    default   3         2020-08-11  deployed  drupal-7.0.0        9.0.0
wordpress default   3         2020-08-12  failed    wordpress-9.3.11  5.4.2
```

It is worth noting again that the REVISION field for our newly failed wordpress installation has been incremented from 2 to 3. Even failed releases have revisions attached to them. We'll see why this is important in "History and Rollbacks" on page 52.

Find Details of a Release with helm get

While helm list provides a summary view of installations, the helm get set of commands provide deeper information about a particular release.

There are five helm get subcommands (hooks, manifests, notes, values, and all). Each subcommand retrieves some portion of the information Helm tracks for a release.

Using helm get notes

The helm get notes subcommand prints the release notes:

```
$ helm get notes mysite
NOTES:

*********************************************************************
*** PLEASE BE PATIENT: Drupal may take a few minutes to install ***
*********************************************************************

1. Get the Drupal URL:

   You should be able to access your new Drupal installation through

   http://drupal.local/
...
```

This output should look familiar, as helm install and helm upgrade both print the release notes at the end of a successful operation. But helm get notes provides a convenient way to grab these notes on demand. That is useful in cases where you've forgotten what the URL is to your Drupal site.

Using helm get values

One useful subcommand is values. You can use this to see which values were supplied during the last release. In the previous section, we upgraded a WordPress installation and caused it to fail. We can see what values caused it to fail using helm get values:

```
$ helm get values wordpress
USER-SUPPLIED VALUES:
image:
  pullPolicy: NoSuchPolicy
```

We know that revision 2 was successful, but revision 3 failed. So we can take a look at the earlier values to see what changed:

```
$ helm get values wordpress --revision 2
USER-SUPPLIED VALUES:
image:
  tag: latest
```

With this, we can see that one value was removed and one value was added. Features like this are designed to make it easier for Helm users to identify the source of errors.

This command is also useful for learning about the total state of a release's configuration. We can use helm get values to see *all* of the values currently set for that release. To do this, we use the --all flag:

```
$ helm get values wordpress --all
COMPUTED VALUES:
affinity: {}
allowEmptyPassword: true
allowOverrideNone: false
customHTAccessCM: null
customLivenessProbe: {}
customReadinessProbe: {}
externalDatabase:
  database: bitnami_wordpress
  host: localhost
  password: ""
  port: 3306
...
```

When the --all flag is specified, Helm will get the complete computed set of values, sorted alphabetically. This is a great tool for seeing the exact state of configuration for the release.

Seeing Default Values

Although helm get values does not have a way of showing you the default values, you can see those with helm inspect values CHARTNAME. This inspects the chart itself (not the release) and prints out the documented default *values.yaml* file. Thus, we could use helm inspect values bitnami/wordpress to see the default configuration for the WordPress chart.

Using helm get manifest

The last helm get subcommand that we will cover is helm get manifest. This subcommand retrieves the exact YAML manifest that Helm produced using the Chart templates:

```
$ helm get manifest wordpress
# Source: wordpress/charts/mariadb/templates/secrets.yaml
apiVersion: v1
kind: Secret
metadata:
  name: wordpress-mariadb
  labels:
    app: "mariadb"
    chart: "mariadb-7.5.1"
    release: "wordpress"
    heritage: "Helm"
type: Opaque
...
```

One important detail about this command is that it does not return the *current state* of all of your resources. It returns *the manifest generated from the template*. In the preceding example, we see a `Secret` named `wordpress-mariadb`. If we query that `Secret` using `kubectl`, the `metadata` section looks like this:

```
$ kubectl get secret wordpress-mariadb -o yaml
apiVersion: v1
kind: Secret
metadata:
  annotations:
    meta.helm.sh/release-name: wordpress
    meta.helm.sh/release-namespace: default
  creationTimestamp: "2020-08-12T16:45:00Z"
  labels:
    app: mariadb
    app.kubernetes.io/managed-by: Helm
    chart: mariadb-7.5.1
    heritage: Helm
    release: wordpress
  managedFields:
  - apiVersion: v1
    fieldsType: FieldsV1
  ...
```

The output of `kubectl` contains the record as it currently exists in Kubernetes. There are several fields that have been added since the template output. Some (like the annotations) are managed by Helm itself, and others (like `managedFields` and `creationTimestamp`) are managed by Kubernetes.

Once again, Helm provides tools designed to ease debugging. Between `helm get manifest` and `kubectl get`, you have tools for comparing what Kubernetes thinks is the current object with what the chart produced. This is particularly helpful when a resource that should be managed by Helm was manually edited outside of Helm (e.g., using `kubectl edit`).

With `helm get`, we can closely inspect an individual release. But the next tool we will cover provides us a view of the progression of releases. In the next section, we will look at `helm history` and `helm rollback`.

History and Rollbacks

Throughout this book, we have distinguished between installations and revisions. In this chapter, we have been working with an installation named `mysite` and another installation named `wordpress`. And when we ran `helm list` earlier, we saw that each installation had three releases. Moreover, we saw that `wordpress` was in a failed state:

```
$ helm list
NAME        NAMESPACE REVISION  UPDATED     STATUS    CHART            APP VER...
mysite      default   3         2020-08-11  deployed  drupal-7.0.0     9.0.0
wordpress   default   3         2020-08-12  failed    wordpress-9.3.11 5.4.2
```

We can investigate the release history of WordPress to see what happened. To do this, we will use `helm history`:

```
$ helm history wordpress
REVISION UPDATED      STATUS      CHART            APP VER  DESCRIPTION
1        Wed Aug 12... superseded wordpress-9.3.11 5.4.2    Install complete
2        Wed Aug 12... deployed   wordpress-9.3.11 5.4.2    Upgrade complete
3        Wed Aug 12... failed     wordpress-9.3.11 5.4.2    Upgrade \
   "wordpress" failed: cannot patch "wordpress" with kind Deployment: \
   Deployment.apps "wordpress" is invalid: \
   spec.template.spec.containers[0].imagePullPolicy: Unsupported value: \
   "NoSuchPolicy": supported values: "Always", "IfNotPresent", "Never"
```

The output of this command gives us a nice history of the `wordpress` release. First it was installed, and then it was upgraded and marked deployed (which means that it was a successful upgrade). But when it was upgraded again, that upgrade `failed`. The `helm history` command even gives us the error message that Kubernetes returned when marking the release `failed`.

From the error, we know that the release failed because we supplied an invalid image pull policy. So of course we could correct this by simply running another `helm upgrade`. But imagine a case where the cause of error was not readily available. Rather than leave the application in a failed state while diagnosing the problem, it would be nice to simply revert back to the release that worked before.

This is what `helm rollback` is for:

```
$ helm rollback wordpress 2
Rollback was a success! Happy Helming!
```

This command tells Helm to fetch the `wordpress` version 2 release, and resubmit that manifest to Kubernetes. A rollback does *not* restore to a previous snapshot of the cluster. Helm does not track enough information to do that. What it does is resubmit the previous configuration, and Kubernetes attempts to reset the resources to match.

Now we can once again use `helm history` to see what has happened:

```
REVISION  UPDATED        STATUS      CHART            APP VER  DESCRIPTION
1         Wed Aug 12... superseded  wordpress-9.3.11 5.4.2    Install complete
2         Wed Aug 12... superseded  wordpress-9.3.11 5.4.2    Upgrade complete
3         Wed Aug 12... failed      wordpress-9.3.11 5.4.2    Upgrade \
   "wordpress" failed: cannot patch "wordpress" with kind Deployment: \
   Deployment.apps "wordpress" is invalid: \
   spec.template.spec.containers[0].imagePullPolicy: Unsupported value: \
   "NoSuchPolicy": supported values: "Always", "IfNotPresent", "Never"
4         Wed Aug 12... deployed    wordpress-9.3.11 5.4.2    Rollback to 2
```

The rollback operation created a new revision (4). Since the rollback was successful (and Kubernetes accepted the alterations), the release is marked `deployed`. Note that revision 2 is now marked `superseded`, while the failed release 3 is still marked `failed`.

Because Helm has preserved the history, you can still examine the failed release after rolling back to a known-good configuration.

In most cases, `helm rollback` is a great way to recover from a catastrophe. But if you hand-edit resources that are managed by Helm, an interesting problem may arise. Rollbacks can on occasion cause some unexpected behavior, especially if the Kubernetes resources have been hand-edited by users. Helm and Kubernetes will attempt to preserve those hand-edits if they do not conflict with the rollback. Essentially, a rollback will generate a 3-way diff between the current state of the resources, the failed Helm release, and the Helm release that you roll back to. In some cases, the generated diff may result in rolling back handmade edits, while in other cases those discrepancies will be merged. In the worst case, some handmade edits may be overwritten while other related edits are merged, leading to an inconsistency in configuration. This is one of the many reasons Helm core maintainers recommend against hand-editing resources. If all edits are made through Helm, then you can use Helm tools effectively and with no guesswork.

Keeping History and Rolling Back

In the previous chapter, we saw that the `helm uninstall` command has a flag called `--keep-history`. Normally, a deletion event will destroy all release records associated with that installation. But when `--keep-history` is specified, you can see the history of an installation even after it has been deleted:

```
$ helm uninstall wordpress --keep-history
release "wordpress" uninstalled
```

```
$ helm history wordpress
REVISION UPDATED       STATUS       CHART            APP V  DESCRIPTION
1        Wed Aug 12... superseded   wordpress-9.3.11 5.4.2  Install complete
2        Wed Aug 12... superseded   wordpress-9.3.11 5.4.2  Upgrade complete
3        Wed Aug 12... failed       wordpress-9.3.11 5.4.2  Upgrade \
  "wordpress" failed: cannot patch "wordpress" with kind Deployment: \
  Deployment.apps "wordpress" is invalid: \
  spec.template.spec.containers[0].imagePullPolicy: Unsupported value: \
  "NoSuchPolicy": supported values: "Always", "IfNotPresent", "Never"
4        Wed Aug 12... uninstalled  wordpress-9.3.11 5.4.2  Uninstall complete
```

Note that the last release is now marked as uninstalled. When history is preserved, you can roll back a deleted installation:

```
$ helm rollback wordpress 4
Rollback was a success! Happy Helming!
```

And now we can see a newly deployed release 5:

```
$ helm history wordpress
REVISION UPDATED     STATUS       CHART              APP VER  DESCRIPTION
1        Wed Aug... superseded   wordpress-9.3.11      5.4.2     Install complete
2        Wed Aug... superseded   wordpress-9.3.11      5.4.2     Upgrade complete
3        Wed Aug... failed       wordpress-9.3.11      5.4.2     Upgrade \
  "wordpress" failed: cannot patch "wordpress" with kind Deployment: \
  Deployment.apps "wordpress" is invalid: \
  spec.template.spec.containers[0].imagePullPolicy: Unsupported value: \
  "NoSuchPolicy": supported values: "Always", "IfNotPresent", "Never"
4        Wed Aug... uninstalled wordpress-9.3.11 5.4.2   Uninstall complete
5        Wed Aug... deployed    wordpress-9.3.11 5.4.2   Rollback to 4
```

But without the --keep-history flag, this will not work:

```
$ helm uninstall wordpress
release "wordpress" uninstalled
$ helm history wordpress
Error: release: not found
$ helm rollback wordpress 4
Error: release: not found
```

A Deep Dive into Installs and Upgrades

In Chapter 2 we took a first look at installing and upgrading Helm packages, and throughout this chapter we have looked at tools that help us work with Helm installations. To close out this chapter, we will circle back to installation and upgrading and look at a few advanced features.

The --generate-name and --name-template Flags

One of the subtle dangers of the way Kubernetes works has to do with naming. Kubernetes assumes that names will have certain uniqueness properties. For example, a `Deployment` object must have a name unique within its namespace. That is, in the namespace `mynamespace` I cannot have two `Deployments` named `myapp`. But I can have a `Deployment` and a `Pod` each named `myapp`.

This has made certain tasks a little more complicated. For example, a CI system that automatically deploys things must be able to ensure that the name it gives these things is unique within the namespace. One approach to dealing with this issue is for Helm to provide a tool for generating a unique name. (Another approach is to always overwrite a name if it already exits. See the next section for that approach.)

Helm provides the `--generate-name` flag for `helm install`:

```
$ helm install bitnami/wordpress --generate-name
NAME: wordpress-1597689085
LAST DEPLOYED: Mon Aug 17 11:31:27 2020
NAMESPACE: default
STATUS: deployed
REVISION: 1
```

With the `--generate-name` flag, we no longer need to provide a name as the first argument to `helm install`. Helm generates a name based on a combination of the chart name and a timestamp. In the preceding output, we can see the name that was generated for us: `wordpress-1597689085`.

In Helm 2, "friendly names" were generated using adjectives and animal names. That was removed in Helm 3 due to complaints that release names were unprofessional. There is currently no way to re-enable this feature.

However, there is an additional flag that allows you to specify a naming template. The `--name-template` flag allows you do to something like this:

```
$ helm install bitnami/wordpress --generate-name \
  --name-template "foo-{{ randAlpha 9 | lower }}"
NAME: foo-yejpiyjmp
LAST DEPLOYED: Mon Aug 17 11:46:04 2020
NAMESPACE: default
```

In this example, we used the name template `foo-{{ randAlpha 9 | lower }}`. This uses the Helm template engine to generate a name for you. We'll cover the Helm template engine in the next few chapters. But here's what the name template does: The `{{` and `}}` demarcate the beginning and end of a template. Inside of that template, we are calling the `randAlpha` function, asking for a 9-character random string from the `a-z`, `A-Z` range of characters. Then we are "piping" the results through a second function (`lower`) that lowercases everything.

Looking at the output of the earlier example, the result of `{{ randAlpha 9 | lower }}` was `yejpiyjmp`. So the result of the entire name template was `foo-yejpiyjmp`.

The --create-namespace Flag

Another consideration with naming in Kubernetes has to do with namespaces. Earlier, we saw that no two objects of the same kind *within the same namespace* can have the same name. But Kubernetes also has a concept of global names. CRDs and namespaces each have global names.

A namespace, therefore, must be unique cluster-wide.

Whenever Helm encounters globally unique names, it adopts a defensive posture. In later chapters, we'll see how charts handle globally unique names. But here, it is worth pointing out that Helm 3 assumes by default that if you attempt to deploy a chart into a namespace, that namespace was already created.

For example, on a fresh cluster this will fail:

```
$ helm install drupal bitnami/drupal --namespace mynamespace
Error: create: failed to create: namespaces "mynamespace" not found
```

It fails because `mynamespace` has not already been created and *Helm won't automatically create a namespace.* It won't create one because namespaces are global, and the safe assumption is that when a namespace is created, it probably needs access controls (like RBACs) and other things assigned to it before it can be safely used in production. In short, it views silently creating a namespace as an opportunity for unintentionally creating a security hole.

However, Helm does let you override this consideration by explicitly stating that you want to create a namespace:

```
$ helm install drupal bitnami/drupal --namespace mynamespace --create-namespace
NAME: drupal
LAST DEPLOYED: Mon Aug 17 11:59:29 2020
NAMESPACE: mynamespace
STATUS: deployed
```

By adding `--create-namespace`, we have indicated to Helm that we *acknowledge* that there may not be a namespace with that name already, and we just want one to be created. Be sure, of course, that if you use this flag on a production instance, you have other mechanisms for enforcing security on this new namespace.

There is not an analogous `--delete-namespace` on `helm uninstall`. And the reason for this falls out of Helm's defensiveness regarding global objects. Once a namespace is created, any number of objects may be put in the namespace, not all of them managed by Helm. And when a namespace is deleted, all of the objects inside of that namespace are also deleted. So Helm does not automatically delete namespaces that were created with `--create-namespace`. To delete a namespace, use `kubectl delete namespace` (after making sure, of course, that no important objects exist in that namespace).

Using helm upgrade --install

Some systems, like CI pipelines, are employed to automatically install or upgrade a chart each time a significant event occurs. For example, many organizations have pipelines that trigger whenever new code is uploaded to a version control system (VCS) like Git. GitHub, a popular Git hosting service, even provides tools to automatically deploy whenever a code change is merged.

Systems like this often run rudimentary scripts on a stateless platform that does not have the means to query Kubernetes. Users of such systems requested a Helm feature that would allow "install or upgrade" support in a single command.

To facilitate this behavior, Helm maintainers added the `--install` flag to the `helm upgrade` command. The `helm upgrade --install` command will install a release if it does not exist already, or will upgrade a release if a release by that name is found. Underneath the hood, it works by querying Kubernetes for a release with the given name. If that release does not exist, it switches out of the upgrade logic and into the install logic.

For example, we can run an install and an upgrade in sequence using exactly the same command:

```
$ helm upgrade --install wordpress bitnami/wordpress
Release "wordpress" does not exist. Installing it now.
NAME: wordpress
LAST DEPLOYED: Mon Aug 17 13:18:14 2020
NAMESPACE: default
STATUS: deployed
...
$ helm upgrade --install wordpress bitnami/wordpress
Release "wordpress" has been upgraded. Happy Helming!
NAME: wordpress
LAST DEPLOYED: Mon Aug 17 13:18:43 2020
NAMESPACE: default
STATUS: deployed
```

As we can see in the first line of output, the first run of the command caused an install, while the second caused an upgrade.

This command does introduce some danger, though. Helm has no way of establishing whether the name of the installation you provide to `helm upgrade --install` belongs to the release you intend to upgrade or just *happens* to be the named the same thing as the thing you want to install. Careless use of this command could result in overwriting one installation with another. This is why it is not the default behavior for Helm.

The --wait and --atomic Flags

Another pair of significant flags for `helm install` and `helm upgrade` modify the success criteria for Helm operations. These are the `--wait` and `--atomic` flags.

The `--wait` flag modifies the behavior of the Helm client in a couple of ways. First, when Helm runs an installation, it remains active for a set window of time (modifiable with the `--timeout` flag) during which it watches Kubernetes. It polls the Kubernetes API server for information about all pod-running objects that were created by the chart. For example, `DaemonSets`, `Deployments`, and `StatefulSets` all create pods. So Helm with `--wait` will track such objects, waiting until the pods they create are marked as `Running` by Kubernetes.

In a normal install or upgrade, Helm marks a release as successful as soon as the Kubernetes API server accepts the manifests. This is similar to package managers that consider a package successfully installed as soon as the package contents are written to the correct storage locations.

But with `--wait`, the success criteria for an installation is modified. A chart is not considered successfully installed unless (1) the Kubernetes API server accepts the manifest and (2) all of the pods created by the chart reach the `Running` state before Helm's timeout expires.

Thus, installs with `--wait` can fail for a wide variety of reasons, including network latency, a slow scheduler, busy nodes, slow image pulls, and outright failure of a container to start.

This behavior is seen as a desirable outcome, and operators use `helm install --wait` to ensure that not only did the chart successfully install but that the resulting application correctly started. However, it does introduce some complicating factors when troubleshooting. Transient outages may result in Helm failures that are resolved by Kubernetes later. For example, a delayed image pull might result in a Helm release marked as failed, even though a few minutes later the image pull can complete and the application can be started.

With this in mind, though, `helm install --wait` is a good tool for making sure that the release is brought all the way to running. But when used in automated systems (like CI), it may cause spurious failures. One recommendation for using `--wait` in CI is to use a long `--timeout` (five or ten minutes) to ensure that Kubernetes has time to resolve any transient failures.

A second strategy is to use the `--atomic` flag instead of the `--wait` flag. This flag causes the same behavior as `--wait` unless the release fails. Then, instead of marking the release as `failed` and exiting, it performs an automatic rollback to the last successful release. In automated systems, the `--atomic` flag is more resistent to outages, since it is less likely to have a failure as its end result. (Keep in mind, though, that there is no assurance that a rollback will be successful.)

Just as `--wait` can mark a release as a failure for transitive reasons that may be resolved by Kubernetes itself, `--atomic` may trigger an unnecessary rollback for the same reasons. Thus, it is recommended to use longer `--timeout` durations for `--atomic`, especially when used with CI systems.

Upgrading with --force and --cleanup-on-fail

The last two flags we will look at modify the way that Helm handles the nuances of upgrades.

The `--force` flag modifies the behavior of Helm when it upgrades a resource that manages pods (like `Pod`, `Deployment`, and `StatefulSet`). Normally, when Kubernetes receives a request to modify such objects, it determines whether it needs to restart the pods that this resource manages. For example, a `Deployment` may run five replicas of a pod. But if Kubernetes receives an update to the `Deployment` object, it will only restart those pods if certain fields are modified.

Sometimes, though, Helm users want to make sure that the pods are restarted. That's where the `--force` flag comes in. Instead of modifying the `Deployment` (or similar object), it will delete and re-create it. This forces Kubernetes to delete the old pods and create new ones. By design, using `--force` will cause downtime. While it is often only seconds of downtime, it is downtime nonetheless. It is recommended to only use `--force` when the situation clearly calls for it, not as a default option. For example, the core maintainers do not recommend using `--force` in CI pipelines that deploy to production.

Another way to modify the behavior of an upgrade is to use the `--cleanup-on-fail` flag. Similarly to `--force`, this flag instructs Helm to do additional work.

Consider the case where you install a chart that creates one Kubernetes `Secret`. A new version of the chart is created, and it creates a second `Secret`. But partway through the installation, Helm encounters an error and marks the release a failure. It is possible for the second `Secret` to be left hanging. This situation is more likely to arise if `--wait` or `--atomic` are used, since those may fail after Kubernetes has accepted the manifests and created the resources.

The `--cleanup-on-fail` flag will attempt to fix this situation. On failure, it will request deletion on every object that was *newly created* during the upgrade. Using it may make it a little harder to debug (especially if the failure was a result of the newly created object), but it is useful if you do not want to risk having unused objects hanging around after a failure.

Conclusion

The Helm command-line tool provides many useful commands. While the basic commands were introduced in the previous chapter, this chapter has focused on some of the other useful commands in Helm. Near the end, we also revisited the installation and upgrade commands, getting a taste of some of the more sophisticated features for working with those.

However, not all of the commands were discussed here. In coming chapters, we'll take a look at commands for creating and packaging charts, commands for signing and verifying packages, and more commands for working with repositories.

## CHAPTER 4

Building a Chart

Charts are at the heart of Helm. In addition to installing them into a Kubernetes cluster or managing the instances of charts you've installed, you can build new charts or alter existing ones. In the next three chapters we will cover a lot of details about charts including creating them, the elements inside them, templating Kubernetes manifests, testing charts, dependencies, and more.

In this chapter you will learn how to create a new chart and learn about the many parts of a chart. This will include the use of several built-in commands that can help you in the chart development process.

Charts are the packages Helm works with. They are conceptually similar to Debian packages used by APT or Formula used by Homebrew for macOS. The conceptual similarity is where the similarities end. Charts are designed to target Kubernetes as a platform that has its own unique style. At the heart of charts are templates to generate Kubernetes manifests that can be installed and managed in a cluster.

Before we dig into templates in Chapter 5, let's start by creating a basic fully functional chart. To do that we will cover an example chart named *anvil*. Using that chart you will learn about using Helm to generate a chart, the structure of charts and files within them, packaging charts, and linting charts. Reference the online source for this chart at *https://github.com/Masterminds/learning-helm/tree/main/chapter4/anvil*.

The Chart Creation Command

Helm includes the `create` command to make it easy for you to create a chart of your own, and it's a great way to get started. This command creates a new Nginx chart, with a name of your choice, following best practices for a chart layout. Since Kubernetes clusters can have different methods to expose an application, this chart makes the way Nginx is exposed to network traffic configurable so it can be exposed in a wide variety of clusters.

The `create` command creates a chart for you, with all the required chart structure and files. These files are documented to help you understand what is needed, and the templates it provides showcase multiple Kubernetes manifests working together to deploy an application. In addition, you can install and test this chart right out of the box.

Throughout this chapter we will look at an example application named *anvil*. It is a simple application that will show you the structure of a chart and provide you the chance to alter a chart for a different application. To create the new chart, run the following command from a command prompt:

```
$ helm create anvil
```

This will create a new chart as a subdirectory of your current directory with the name *anvil*.

Different Starting Points

Nginx is a good starting point to showcase the parts of a chart and for basic stateless services. However, if you regularly create charts that do not follow the Nginx model, a different starting point would be more helpful. For this purpose, Helm has a feature called *starter packs*, which `helm create` can utilize to provide a different starting point to generate a chart from. This is covered in Chapter 6.

The new chart is a directory containing a number of files and folders. This does not include every file and folder—you will discover some more in the next couple chapters. These are the basic ones needed for a functioning chart:

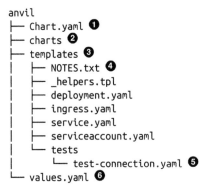

❶   The *Chart.yaml* file contains metadata and some functionality controls for the chart.

---

❷ Dependent charts can optionally be held in the *charts* directory. Chart dependencies are covered in Chapter 6. For now this will be an empty directory.

❸ Templates used to generate Kubernetes manifests are stored in the *templates* directory.

❹ The *NOTES.txt* file is a special template. When a chart is installed, the *NOTES.txt* template is rendered and displayed rather than being installed into a cluster.

❺ Templates can include tests that are not installed as part of the `install` or `upgrade` commands. This chart includes a test that is used by the `helm test` command. Testing is covered in Chapter 6.

❻ Default values passed to the templates when Helm is rendering the manifests are in the *values.yaml* file. When you instantiate a chart, these values can be overridden.

You can install this newly created chart without any modifications by running the following command:

```
$ helm install myapp anvil
```

When you run this command Helm will create an instance of the chart running in the cluster with the name *myapp*. It will install it using the currently configured connection and context you use for Kubernetes. Helm is using the same configuration you're using when you use `kubectl`, the command-line application for Kubernetes. In that command the final argument of *anvil* is the directory where the chart is located.

The output from this command includes content generated by rendering the *NOTES.txt* template, as shown here:

```
NAME: myapp
LAST DEPLOYED: Sun Apr  5 08:12:59 2020
NAMESPACE: default
STATUS: deployed
REVISION: 1
NOTES:
1. Get the application URL by running these commands:
   export POD_NAME=$(kubectl get pods --namespace default ↵
     -l "app.kubernetes.io/name=anvil,app.kubernetes.io/instance=myapp" ↵
     -o jsonpath="{.items[0].metadata.name}")
   echo "Visit http://127.0.0.1:8080 to use your application"
   kubectl --namespace default port-forward $POD_NAME 8080:80
```

The NOTES section contains information on connecting to the application. Depending on the values you pass into the chart when it is instantiated, this information can be very different. This chart can be configured to use a ClusterIP, NodePort, LoadBalancer, and Ingress to expose an application. By default, a ClusterIP is used.

If you follow the directions in the notes you will see the default Nginx web page to show you it's running, as shown in Figure 4-1.

Figure 4-1. Default Nginx web page when you visit the running application

The methods to expose the application are tied to built-in Kubernetes resource types rather than features of the application. That makes them portable to your custom applications. The methods to expose applications include:

ClusterIP

A configuration option on the Kubernetes `Service` resource type that exposes the service on a cluster-level internal IP address.

NodePort

An alternative option for Kubernetes `Service` resources that exposes the service on a static port of each node. A ClusterIP is automatically created as well.

LoadBalancer

A Kubernetes `Service` configuration option that exposes an application externally using a load balancer provided by the hosting provider.

Ingress

Ingress resources are additional resources to `Services` that expose a service over HTTP and HTTPS. An Ingress Controller, such as ingress-nginx, is required for this to work.

If you installed this chart into your cluster to test it, you can delete the instance from your cluster by running the following command:

```
$ helm delete myapp
```

When the chart is installed the image used for Nginx, by default, is the latest version of the image from the Docker Official Images (*https://oreil.ly/YghQP*). If the Kubernetes cluster you are working with does not have access to *hub.docker.com* you won't be able to install the image. You would need to set the image to one your cluster has access to.

Now that a working chart has been scaffolded, let's take a look at what's inside and modify it for the Anvil application.

The Chart.yaml File

Look inside the *anvil* directory and you'll find a file named *Chart.yaml*. The *Chart.yaml* file tells Helm and other tools about your chart. Other tools include Kubeapps (an on-premise catalog and application installer), the Artifact Hub (a listing of cloud native artifacts), and many others.

When you open the *Chart.yaml* file, you will see the contents shown in Example 4-1.

Example 4-1. The generated Chart.yaml file

```
apiVersion: v2 ❶
name: anvil ❷
description: A Helm chart for Kubernetes

# A chart can be either an 'application' or a 'library' chart.
#
# Application charts are a collection of templates that can be packaged into ↵
  versioned archives
# to be deployed.
#
# Library charts provide useful utilities or functions for the chart developer.↵
  They're included as
# a dependency of application charts to inject those utilities and functions ↵
  into the rendering
# pipeline. Library charts do not define any templates and therefore cannot be ↵
  deployed.
type: application

# This is the chart version. This version number should be incremented each ↵
  time you make changes
# to the chart and its templates, including the app version.
version: 0.1.0 ❸

# This is the version number of the application being deployed. This version ↵
  number should be
# incremented each time you make changes to the application. Versions are not ↵
  expected to
```

```
# follow Semantic Versioning. They should reflect the version the application ↵
  is using.
appVersion: 1.16.0
```

❶ The `apiVersion` tells Helm what structure the chart is using. An `apiVerison` of
    v2 is designed for Helm v3.

❷ The name is used to identify the chart in various places.

❸ Charts can have many versions. Helm uses the version information to order and
    identify charts.

This *Chart.yaml* file contains numerous keys, of which only three are required. The
`apiVersion` property tells Helm which version of a chart this is. Helm v3 can work
with charts whose `apiVersion` is v1 or v2. v1 charts are those designed to work with
previous versions of Helm. If your charts are designed to work with Helm v3 or
newer you should set this to v2. The value of `name` is typically used as part of the
name for Kubernetes resources. This means names are limited to lowercase alphanumeric, -, and . characters and must start and end with an alphanumeric character.
Names are typically lowercase alphanumeric characters. The final required key is
`version`, containing the version of the chart. Versions are expected to follow Semantic Versioning, which was covered in Chapter 2.

You might notice that the style of a *Chart.yaml* file is similar but mildly different from
those of Kubernetes manifests. *Chart.yaml* files are not the same format as custom
resources but do contain some of the same properties. The original *Chart.yaml* files
were designed back in 2015, long before Kubernetes custom resource definitions existed. While Helm has progressed in major versions, it has maintained a certain
amount of backward compatibility over time to not disrupt users too much. This has
led to differences between the *Chart.yaml* file format and Kubernetes manifests.

Chart.yaml files also contain descriptive information, which is useful as it's presented
in user interfaces. The `description` field in Example 4-1 is one such field, but you
can add additional fields, such as the following:

• `home` is a URL to the chart or projects homepage.

• `icon` is an image (e.g., PNG or SVG file) in the form of a URL.

• `maintainers` contains a list of maintainers. Each maintainer on the list can have
  a name, email, and URL.

• `keywords` can hold a list of keywords about the project.

• `sources` is for a list of URLs to source code for the project or chart.

A full description of the properties in the *Chart.yaml* file are available in Appendix A, for reference.

The generated *Chart.yaml* file can be modified for the Anvil application. The following modifications update the required fields, add some descriptive files, and remove comments:

```
apiVersion: v2
name: anvil
description: A surprise to catch something speedy.
version: 0.1.0
appVersion: 9.17.49
icon: https://wile.example.com/anvil.svg
keywords:
  - road runner
  - anvil
home: https://wile.example.com/
sources:
  - https://github.com/Masterminds/learning-helm/tree/main/chapter4/anvil
maintainers:
  - name: ACME Corp
    email: maintainers@example.com
  - name: Wile E. Coyote
    email: wile@example.com
```

One property that was in the generated *Chart.yaml* file but is not in the one for Anvil is type. Anvil is an application which is the default value for the type field, so the type field is not required. The other type of chart is a library chart, which is covered in Chapter 7.

The appVersion property is unique. It is both descriptive and regularly used within the templates. The appVersion property represents the version of the primary or combined application. For example, if the application being packaged was Word-Press, it would be the version of WordPress.

> The icon property is a URL, and that can include data URLs. Data URLs (*https://oreil.ly/1gj45*) enable you to embed small files in URL form. This is especially useful if the logo is a small SVG file. If a chart may be run in air-gapped on-premise environments or you do not want user interfaces constantly downloading a file from your web server, a data URL is a useful choice.

Modifying Templates

In order to modify this chart for the Anvil application or your own custom application, you will need to understand and modify templates. Out of the box, the templates created by the `helm create` command run Nginx as a stateless application. In the example we are working through, Nginx will need to be replaced with Anvil.

Helm is written in the Go programming language, and Go includes template packages. Helm leverages the text template package as the foundation for its templates. This template language is similar to other template languages and includes loops, if/then logic, functions, and more. An example template of a YAML file follows:

```
product: {{ .Values.product | default "rocket" | quote }}
```

In this YAML file there is a key name of `product`. The value is generated using a template. `{{` and `}}` are the opening and closing brackets to enter and exit template logic. There are three parts to the template logic separated by a `|`. This is called a pipeline, and it works the same way as a pipeline in Unix-based systems. The value or output of a function on the left is passed in as the last argument to the next item in the pipeline. In this case, the pipeline starts with the value from the property in `.Values.product`. This comes from the data object passed in when the templates are rendered. The value of this data is piped as the last argument to the `default` function, which is one of the functions provided by Helm. If the value passed in is empty, the `default` function uses the default value of `"rocket"`, ensuring there is a value. This is then sent to the `quote` function, which ensures the string is wrapped in quotes before writing it to the template.

The `.` at the start of `.Values.product` is important. This is considered the root object in the current scope. `.Values` is a property on the root object.

The Deployment

Helm charts can hold templates for any Kubernetes resource type you might use. That includes `StatefulSets`, `Jobs`, `PersistentVolumeClaims`, `Services`, and much more. The chart created with `helm create` is designed to run a stateless service as a Kubernetes Deployment. The example application we are using here for Anvil is a stateless application, which means it will work well as a deployment.

To understand the `Deployment` template, we can take a look at the *deployment.yaml* file in the *templates* directory of the chart. The following is the templated version of the `Deployment` up to the `spec` section:

```
apiVersion: apps/v1
kind: Deployment
metadata:
  name: {{ include "anvil.fullname" . }}
  labels:
    {{- include "anvil.labels" . | nindent 4 }}
```

This looks very similar to the start of a Kubernetes manifest. It has an `apiVersion`, the `kind`, and `metadata`. Once you get into the `metadata` you'll notice the templating begins.

 If you are unfamiliar with the structure of Kubernetes Deployments, you can read about them in the Kubernetes documentation (*https://oreil.ly/aIuIE*).

The `include` template function enables including the output of one template in another template, and this works in pipelines. The first argument to the `include` function is the name of the template to use. The . passed in as the second argument is the root object. This is passed in so the properties and functions on the root object can be used within the called template.

anvil.fullname and *anvil.labels* are two reusable templates included in the chart via the *_helpers.tpl* file. (The _ at the start of the name causes it to bubble up to the top of directory listings so you can easily find it among your templates; Helm does not render them into Kubernetes manifests but does make templates in them available for use.) *anvil.fullname* provides a name based on the name chosen when the chart is instantiated, and *anvil.labels* provides labels following Kubernetes best practices. The functions are covered in more depth in Chapter 5.

After the `metadata` section of the template is the `spec` section, which reads as follows:

```
spec:
  replicas: {{ .Values.replicaCount }}
  selector:
    matchLabels:
      {{- include "anvil.selectorLabels" . | nindent 6 }}
  template:
    metadata:
      labels:
        {{- include "anvil.selectorLabels" . | nindent 8 }}
    spec:
    {{- with .Values.imagePullSecrets }}
      imagePullSecrets:
        {{- toYaml . | nindent 8 }}
    {{- end }}
      serviceAccountName: {{ include "anvil.serviceAccountName" . }}
      securityContext:
        {{- toYaml .Values.podSecurityContext | nindent 8 }}
      containers:
        - name: {{ .Chart.Name }}
          securityContext:
            {{- toYaml .Values.securityContext | nindent 12 }}
          image: "{{ .Values.image.repository }}:{{ .Values.image.tag | default↵
            .Chart.AppVersion }}" ❶
```

```
          imagePullPolicy: {{ .Values.image.pullPolicy }}
          ports:
            - name: http
              containerPort: 80
              protocol: TCP
          livenessProbe:
            httpGet:
              path: /
              port: http
          readinessProbe:
            httpGet:
              path: /
              port: http
          resources:
            {{- toYaml .Values.resources | nindent 12 }}
      {{- with .Values.nodeSelector }}
      nodeSelector:
        {{- toYaml . | nindent 8 }}
      {{- end }}
    {{- with .Values.affinity }}
      affinity:
        {{- toYaml . | nindent 8 }}
    {{- end }}
    {{- with .Values.tolerations }}
      tolerations:
        {{- toYaml . | nindent 8 }}
    {{- end }}
```

❶ The location and version of the container image is configurable via values.

The spec section completes the deployment. Most of this section is filling in data with the properties on .Values. There are a few elements that are hardcoded, such as the ports used to expose the application. Anvil is exposed over HTTP on port 80, so we do not need to change the port. If your containers are exposed on different ports, you will need to make changes here.

The value of image for the container is set using values. You won't find the location of the image hardcoded here. This is useful for those cases where the image location needs to be set to a different location when a chart is instantiated. It means we need to change the location in the default values.

The properties on .Values are computed based on a number of factors. The default values and starting point are based on the values provided by the *values.yaml* file in the chart. The *values.yaml* file is covered in the next section. These values can be overridden by values passed in when the chart is instantiated. The *helm* CLI has flags to pass in values directly (i.e., --set, --set-file, and --set-string) or to pass in a file with values (i.e., -f or --values). The values are merged together, with those being passed in later taking precedence.

Templates are a large topic and typically make up the bulk of a chart. Chapter 5 is dedicated to templates.

Using the Values File

When someone instantiates an application in a Kubernetes cluster from a chart, they don't need to supply all the values used in the templates. If they did, it would provide for a difficult user experience. This is where the *values.yaml* file comes in.

Charts include a *values.yaml* file that sits alongside the *Chart.yaml* file in the root of a chart. The *values.yaml* file contains the default values used by the chart, and it is a form of documentation for the custom values that can be passed into a chart.

values.yaml is an unstructured YAML file. There are some common and useful practices, which will be covered shortly, but nothing is required in the format of the YAML. This enables chart creators to provide a structure and information that works well for them. A *values.yaml* file can contain numerous things, from simple substitution for Kubernetes manifest properties to elements needed for application-specific business logic.

Container Images

The opening part of the *values.yaml* file created by `helm create` contains the image information along with some opening documentation and information on replicas:

```
# Default values for anvil.
# This is a YAML-formatted file.
# Declare variables to be passed into your templates.

replicaCount: 1

image:
  repository: ghcr.io/masterminds/learning-helm/anvil-app ❶
  pullPolicy: IfNotPresent ❷
  # Overrides the image tag whose default is the chart version.
  tag: "" ❸

imagePullSecrets: [] ❹
```

❶ The location of the image. It has been updated to reflect the location of Anvil.

❷ A policy of `IfNotPresent` means that the image will be cached in the Kubernetes cluster by the version being used. `Always` is another option that bypasses the cache and always downloads from the repository.

❸ By default this chart uses the `appVersion` as the tag. If an image tag is specified, it is used instead of the `appVersion`.

❹ A list of pull secrets is used when credentials are needed to access a container registry location that is protected with a username and password.

This chart and the values represent an application bundled as a single image. The patterns used in the *values.yaml* file are designed with that in mind. For example, there is only one image location. If your applications have multiple images, each image would have a section containing much of the information here. This includes `replicaCount`, which is the number of `replicas` Kubernetes will use when the `Deployment` is created.

The `image` section contains details about the image. The `repository` contains the location of the image to use while the `pullPolicy` tells Kubernetes how often to fetch or cache the images. If a moving tag, such as `stable`, is used, the `pullPolicy` should be set to `Always` so that changes are picked up. Since a version is being used, the default `pullPolicy` is set to `IfNotPresent` so that a cached version can be used if available. The `tag` property provides an opportunity to set a tag that is different from the `appVersion` set in the *Chart.yaml* file.

You might notice there is no method to set a digest when fetching an image. Digests can be different when images are in different repositories. For example, if the Anvil image were copied from Docker Hub to Quay, another image repository, the digest would change for the same image even if the tag and content remained the same. Chapter 5 provides an example of adding in support for a digest to a chart, if that is desired.

If you need to pull an image from a container registry with access controls, Kubernetes needs to know how to do that. This happens through the use of pull secrets. `imagePullSecrets` allows you to list the names of pull secrets with access to private registries. Reference the documentation for creating a pull secret (*https://oreil.ly/BL-VO*).

The generated chart has some security considerations built in that can be enabled or otherwise configured. A service account for the chart instance is created by default, while the other options are opt-in. The following is what is generated by `helm create`:

```
serviceAccount:
  # Specifies whether a service account should be created
  create: true
  # Annotations to add to the service account
  annotations: {}
  # The name of the service account to use.
  # If not set and create is true, a name is generated using the fullname ↵
    template
  name:

podSecurityContext: {}
  # fsGroup: 2000
```

```
securityContext: {}
  # capabilities:
  #   drop:
  #   - ALL
  # readOnlyRootFilesystem: true
  # runAsNonRoot: true
  # runAsUser: 1000
```

You will notice that most of the properties in the configuration are comments and are inactive. When the chart is rendered with the values as comments, there is no value for those properties. The value is empty. By having a structure and values as comments the chart is documenting the structure and default values that can be used but isn't turning on those features.

Exposing Services

The next section of the *values.yaml* file deals with exposing the application for others to consume:

```
service:
  type: ClusterIP
  port: 80

ingress:
  enabled: false
  annotations: {}
    # kubernetes.io/ingress.class: nginx
    # kubernetes.io/tls-acme: "true"
  hosts:
    - host: chart-example.local
      paths: []
  tls: []
  #  - secretName: chart-example-tls
  #    hosts:
  #      - chart-example.local
```

In Kubernetes there are two built-in objects you can use to expose applications. The first is a Service. The service property will let you select the type of Service being used. While ClusterIP is used by default, other options such as NodePort and LoadBalancer can be used. The few lines of YAML in the service section are paired with the generated *service.yaml* template to create a full Service manifest to upload to Kubernetes.

The second built-in object is the Ingress manifest, which can be paired with a Service, and the chart has the capability to generate them. Ingress configuration provides a means to show off a common pattern found in charts: the use of an enabled property to turn features on and off. In this case ingress.enabled is set to false. When Helm renders the templates and sees a value of false, the Ingress manifest is skipped. This is due to the use of an `if` logic statement in the `Ingress` template found in the generated *ingress.yaml* file.

> ## Ingress Controllers
>
> For a functional ingress setup you need more than an `Ingress` resource in Kubernetes. The `Ingress` resource you can include in a chart connects the Ingress Controller to a `Service`. You will need to have an Ingress Controller running in your cluster because one is not included by default. The Kubernetes community provides the Nginx Ingress Controller (*https://oreil.ly/vc3ed*), which is a good default option.

Resource Limits

When you run applications in production, it is a good practice to set resource limits. This prevents, for example, a memory leak in one container from disrupting other containers. When a chart author creates a chart that others are going to use, they may not know where it will be installed and how many resources will be available there. Could this be installed on a laptop by a developer or someone testing out the chart? Or, might this be installed on large production servers? To handle this variance in environment, the recommendation is to put in resource limits and then turn them into comments. This can be found in the next section of the *values.yaml* file:

```
resources: {}
  # We usually recommend not to specify default resources and to leave this as
  # a conscious choice for the user. This also increases chances charts run on
  # environments with little resources, such as Minikube. If you do want to
  # specify resources, uncomment the following lines, adjust them as necessary,
  # and remove the curly braces after 'resources:'.
  # limits:
  #   cpu: 100m
  #   memory: 128Mi
  # requests:
  #   cpu: 100m
  #   memory: 128Mi
```

Those who install applications use these numbers as recommendations when they instantiate a chart. These numbers are the default values that have been set for a simple Nginx setup as it was generated. They work for the Anvil application. If your application will need different values, you will need to update these.

Workloads have the ability to specify details about where they are executed in a cluster by the settings node selector, tolerations, and affinity. Although these more advanced features are often not used, it is a good idea to include them in a chart for those who need them. The generated *values.yaml* file and templates take this into account. The following example has generated YAML keys for these advanced features. The values are empty by default with an expectation that the person who installs the chart will set values as appropriate for their installation:

```
nodeSelector: {}

tolerations: []

affinity: {}
```

Packaging the Chart

You can package the files and directories of a chart into a single archive file. This is useful for many reasons, including:

- For distribution to other people. One of the powerful aspects of a package manager is where someone with knowledge of running an application packages it up so that others, who don't have intimate knowledge of the platform or application, can run it.
- When a version of an application needs to be taken through a multienvironment test process. An example of this process is where there are development, quality assurance (QA), and production environments and the application needs to pass QA prior to going into production.
- When developing a multiservice application and developers need to run services built or otherwise handled by others as part of their development setup.

In each of these situations it is often simpler to pass around a single file for the chart than a directory structure.

Chart versions bring another wrinkle to the way you distribute and consume charts. You or someone consuming your chart may need to use different versions of the chart. This is why it's useful to store and share different versions using chart repositories or Open Container Initiative (OCI) registries, covered in Chapter 7. In these environments, storing and sharing many files in a collection of directory structures for each version is far from simple.

Helm has the ability to build a chart archive. Each chart archive is a gzipped TAR file with the extension *.tgz*. Any tool that can create, extract, and otherwise work on gzipped TAR files will work with Helm's chart archives.

When Helm generates the archive files, they are named using a pattern of *chart name-version.tgz*. Helm expects this same pattern when consuming them. The *chart name* is the name you will find inside the *Chart.yaml* file and the *version* is the chart version. This enables multiple versions of the same chart to be stored alongside each other. You can package Anvil as an archive by running:

```
$ helm package anvil
```

In this case `anvil` is the path to the location where the *anvil* chart source is located. By default, the `helm package` command will place the archive in the directory you were in when you ran the command.

There are some useful flags you can use when packaging a chart:

`--dependency-update` *(-u)*
> Tells Helm to update the dependent charts prior to creating the archive. This will update the *Chart.lock* file and place a copy of the dependent charts in the *chart* directory. Dependencies are covered in more detail in Chapter 6.

`--destination` *(-d)*
> Enables you to set the location to put the chart archive if it is different from the current working directory.

`--app-version`
> Can be used to set the `appVersion` property of the *Chart.yaml* file. This is especially useful if you create new releases of the chart for each new release of your application running within the container and there is no other change to the chart. Automation can use a flag like this as part of the process to build the new version.

`--version`
> Updates the chart's version. This is useful if you're updating the `appVersion` using the command line as part of the process to package a chart.

Flags for Pretty Good Privacy (PGP) signing charts
> Helm charts can be cryptographically signed and verified. The `package` command has flags for the signing portion of the process, while commands like `install` and `upgrade` have flags for the verification portion of the process. Chapter 6 covers this process.

Sometimes you will have files in a chart directory that you do not want to include in the chart archive. Optionally, in a chart directory there can be a *.helmignore* file. This is similar to a *.gitignore* file for Git. The `helm create` command used earlier created one with the following contents:

```
# Patterns to ignore when building packages.
# This supports shell glob matching, relative path matching, and
# negation (prefixed with !). Only one pattern per line.
.DS_Store
# Common VCS dirs
.git/
.gitignore
.bzr/
.bzrignore
.hg/
.hgignore
```

```
.svn/
# Common backup files
*.swp
*.bak
*.tmp
*.orig
*~
# Various IDEs
.project
.idea/
*.tmproj
.vscode/
```

Many of these extensions and patterns may look familiar because they come from various version control systems and code editors.

When the chart archive is created, you usually don't want to include elements like your version control system data. The *.helmignore* file provides a place to specify what to skip. This file needs to be at the top level of the chart.

Helm is designed to work with the archive files the same way it works with directory structures. Commands like `helm install` and `helm lint`, which will be covered shortly, can be passed an archive file the same way they can be passed a directory.

Linting Charts

When developing charts, especially when working with YAML templates, it can be easy to make a mistake or miss something. To help you catch errors, bugs, style issues, and other suspicious elements, the Helm client includes a linter. This linter can be used during chart development and as part of any testing processes.

To use the linter, use the `lint` command on a chart as a directory or a packaged archive:

```
$ helm lint anvil
==> Linting anvil

1 chart(s) linted, 0 chart(s) failed
```

The first line is the command you run, while the following lines are output by Helm. In this case there were no issues. You could use this command on an archive file like the one in the previous section. To do that, change the `anvil` argument, set to the directory location for the chart, to the archive file *anvil-0.1.0.tgz*.

This command is able to lint multiple charts in a single command. For example, if you had a second chart called *mychart* and wanted to lint it alongside *anvil*, you could run the following command:

```
$ helm lint anvil mychart
```

The three levels of actionable feedback about charts Helm provides are info, warning, and errors. Info-level feedback is informational; charts can be installed with info-level feedback. Info-level feedback causes Helm to have an exit code of 0. Error-level feedback means there is a problem with the chart. If a chart generates an Invalid manifest for Kubernetes, such as YAML being invalid, Helm will generate an error. Errors cause Helm to have a nonzero exit code, which is useful to catch issues in automated testing tools. In the middle are warning messages. These messages address findings that may cause issues. By default, warning messages cause Helm to have an exit code of 0, but Helm adds a `--strict` flag that causes the exit codes to be nonzero. You can choose how to handle these in automation.

Exit Codes

When an application exits, it provides a code or status (*https://oreil.ly/zHz8g*) to the parent that executed it. When you run Helm this is usually the operating system, command prompt, or shell. A zero exit status means that the application exited without any issues. A nonzero exit status means there was a problem. Automated testing systems often use exit codes to know when to continue or stop. Typically, when an application used in automated testing returns a nonzero exit code, the automated processes end and people are notified of an error.

In this case there were no issues found with the *anvil* chart. A default chart, created by `helm create`, will have a single info message about a missing `icon` property in the *Chart.yaml* file. This is an info-level notice so that people are aware it is missing. The missing icon will not affect the operation of the chart, but it will affect the way it is displayed in user interfaces.

Conclusion

Creating a simple chart for your application is straightforward when you use the `helm create` command. Even when your applications are more complicated, the structure of charts is able to accommodate them, and the `helm create` command can help you. With a few minor modifications made in this chapter you can install the Anvil chart using `helm install` and see the custom application running in your cluster. You can use this same flow to create your own charts.

In the next chapter you will learn about creating templates with an emphasis on how the template language works and how you can apply it to Kubernetes templates stored in charts. Templates are usually the largest part of a chart where you will spend the most time. Understanding what you have available to you when you create templates will make the process of developing them faster and easier.

## CHAPTER 5

Developing Templates

Templates are at the heart of Helm charts, and they make up a majority of the files and content of a chart. These are the files that live within the *templates* directory. Helm will render the templates and send them to Kubernetes when you run commands like `helm install` and `helm upgrade`. If you use the `helm template` command, the templates are rendered and displayed as output (i.e., sent to standard out).

The template engine enables a wide range of ways to build templates. In simple situations, you can substitute values in Kubernetes manifest YAML files with values passed in by the user or from the *values.yaml* file. In more complex situations, you can build logic into templates that simplify what chart consumers need to input. Or you can build in features that can configure applications themselves.

In this chapter you will learn how to develop templates and understand how the template syntax works. We'll also cover a number of cool features that Helm has added to the templates that enable you to work with YAML and interact with Kubernetes. Along the way we will look at some patterns you can apply to your own templates.

The Template Syntax

Helm uses the Go text template engine provided as part of the Go standard library. The syntax is used in `kubectl` (the command-line application for Kubernetes) templates, Hugo (the static site generator), and numerous other applications built in Go. The template engine, as it is used in Helm, is designed to work with various types of text files.

You don't need to know the Go programming language to develop templates. There are some Go-isms in the template engine, but if you don't know Go you can treat them as nuances of the template language. We will call them out as you learn to develop templates.

Actions

Logic, control structures, and data evaluations are wrapped by {{ and }}. These are called actions. Anything outside of actions is copied to output.

When the curly brackets are used to start and stop actions they can be accompanied by a - to remove leading or trailing whitespace. The following example illustrates this:

```
{{ "Hello" -}} , {{- "World" }}
```

The generated output of this is "Hello,World." The whitespace has been removed from the side with the - up to the next nonwhitespace character. There needs to be an ASCII whitespace between the - and the rest of the action. For example, {{-12}} evaluates to –12 because the - is considered part of the number instead of the bracket.

Within actions there are a wide variety of features you can leverage, including pipelines, if/else statements, loops, variables, subtemplates, and functions. Using these together provides a powerful way to program templates.

Information Helm Passes to Templates

When Helm renders a template it passes a single data object to the template with information you can access. Inside the template that object is represented as a . (i.e., a period). It is referred to as a dot. This object has a wide variety of information available on it.

In Chapter 4, you already saw how values in the *values.yaml* file are available as properties on .Values. The properties on .Values are specific to each chart based entirely on the values in the *values.yaml* file and those passed into a chart. The properties on .Values do not have a schema and vary from chart to chart.

In addition to the values, information about the release, as first described in Chapter 2, can be accessed as properties of `.Release`. This information includes:

`.Release.Name`
> The name of the release.

`.Release.Namespace`
> Contains the namespace the chart is being released to.

`.Release.IsInstall`
> Set to `true` when the release is a workload being installed.

`.Release.IsUpgrade`
> Set to `true` when the release is an upgrade or rollback.

`.Release.Service`
> Lists the service performing the release. When Helm installs a chart, this value is set to `"Helm"`. Different applications, those that build on Helm, can set this to their own value.

The information in the *Chart.yaml* file can also be found on the data object at `.Chart`. This information does follow the schema for the *Chart.yaml* file. This includes:

`.Chart.Name`
> Contains the name of the chart.

`.Chart.Version`
> The version of the chart.

`.Chart.AppVersion`
> The application version, if set.

`.Chart.Annotations`
> Contains a key/value list of annotations.

Each of the properties that can be in a *Chart.yaml* file is accessible. The names differ in that they start with a lowercase letter in *Chart.yaml* but start with an uppercase letter when they are properties on the `.Chart` object.

If you want to pass custom information from the *Chart.yaml* file to the templates, you need to use annotations. The `.Chart` object only contains the fields from the *Chart.yaml* file that are in the schema. You can't add new fields to pass them in, but you can add your custom information to the annotations.

Different Kubernetes clusters can have different capabilities. This can depend on things like the version of Kubernetes you are using or if there are custom resource definitions (CRDs) installed. Helm provides some data about the capabilities of the cluster as properties of `.Capabilities`. Helm interrogates the cluster you are deploying an application into to get this information. This includes:

`.Capabilities.APIVersions`
> Contains the API versions and resource types available in your cluster. You will learn how to use this in a little bit.

`.Capabilities.KubeVersion.Version`
> The full Kubernetes version.

`.Capabilities.KubeVersion.Major`
> Contains the major Kubernetes version. Because Kubernetes has not been incrementing the major version, this is set to 1.

`.Capabilities.KubeVersion.Minor`
> The minor version of Kubernetes being used in the cluster.

When `helm template` is used, Helm does not interrogate a cluster the same way it does for `helm install` or `helm upgrade`. The capabilities information provided to templates being processed when `helm template` is run is default information Helm already knows about compliant Kubernetes clusters. Helm works this way because the `template` command is expected to only be used for processing templates and doing so in a manner that does not accidentally leak information from a configured cluster.

Charts can contain custom files. For example, you can have a configuration file you want to pass to an application through a `ConfigMap` or `Secret` as a file in the chart. The nonspecial files in a chart that are not listed in the *.helmignore* file are available on `.Files` within templates. This will not give you access to the template files.

The .helmignore File

You can include files in a chart directory that you do not want packaged up in a chart archive and that you do not want to be used by Helm or the chart. List those files in a *.helmignore* file at the root of the chart alongside the *Chart.yaml* file.

A *.helmignore* file is similar to a *.gitignore* file in Git, the source code management system. Individual files, directories, and patterns of files to ignore can be listed. When `helm create` is run to generate a new chart, it includes a *.helmignore* file that ignores common source control management systems and editor files.

The final piece of data passed into the template is details about the current template being executed. Helm passes in:

`.Template.Name`
> Contains the namespaced filepath to the template. For example, in the *anvil* chart from Chapter 4 a path would be *anvil/templates/deployment.yaml*.

`.Template.BasePath`
> The namespaced path to the *templates* directory of the current chart (e.g., *anvil/templates*).

Later in this chapter you will learn how you can change the scope of . in some circumstances. When the scope changes, properties like `.Capabilities.KubeVersion.Minor` will become inaccessible at that location. When template execution begins, . is mapped to $ and $ does not change. Even when the scope changes, `$.Capabilities.KubeVersion.Minor` and other passed-in data is still accessible. You will find $ is typically only used when the scope has changed.

Now that you've learned about the data being passed into the template, we will look at how you can use and manipulate that data within a template.

Pipelines

A pipeline is a sequence of commands, functions, and variables chained together. The value of a variable or the output of a function is used as the input to the next function in a pipeline. The output of the final element of a pipeline is the output of the pipeline. The following illustrates a simple pipeline:

```
character: {{ .Values.character | default "Sylvester" | quote }}
```

There are three parts to this pipeline, each separated by a `|`. The first is `.Values.character`, which is a calculated value of `character`. This is either the value of `character` from the *values.yaml* file or one passed in when the chart is being rendered by `helm install`, `helm upgrade`, or `helm template`. This value is passed as the last argument to the `default` function. If the value is empty, `default` will use the value of "Sylvester" in its place. The output of `default` is passed as an input to `quote`, which ensures the value is wrapped in quotation marks. The output of `quote` is returned from the action.

Pipelines are a powerful tool you can use to transform data you want in the template. They can be used for a variety of purposes, from creating powerful transformations to protecting against simple bugs. Can you spot the bug in the following YAML output?

```
id: 12345e2
```

The value of `id` looks like a string, but it is not. The only letter is an *e*, and the rest are numbers. YAML parsers, including the one used by Kubernetes, will interpret that as a number in scientific notation. This will cause errors. A short string like this is a common output when you get a shortened version of a digest or commit ID from Git. A simple fix is to wrap the value in quotes:

```
id: "12345e2"
```

When the value is wrapped in quotes, the YAML parsers will interpret it as a string. This is a case where using the `quote` function on the end of a pipeline can fix or avoid a bug.

Unix Pipeline

In Unix and Unix-like systems (e.g., Linux) a pipeline is where the output of one application is used as an input in the next application. Applications that each do one thing can be chained together using their inputs and outputs as interfaces.

Pipelines originated from Douglas McIlroy and were later incorporated into the Unix philosophy by Ken Thompson, who worked on the design and implementation of the original Unix operating system. Two principles from the Unix philosophy include "make each program do one thing well" and "expect the output of every program to become the input to another, as yet unknown, program."

Ken Thompson and Rob Pike, another member of the Unix team, are two of the original creators of the Go programming language.

Template Functions

Within actions and pipelines, there are template functions you can use. You have already seen some of these, including the `default` and `quote` functions described earlier in this chapter. Functions provide a means to transform the data you have into the format you need rendered or to generate data where none exists.

Most of the functions are provided by Helm and are designed to be useful when building charts. The functions range from the simple, like the indent and nindent functions used to indent output, to the complex ones that are able to reach into the cluster and get information on current resources and resource types.

Sprig Library

Many of the functions found in Helm templates are provided by a library named Sprig (*https://oreil.ly/fBfwm*). These functions were developed alongside Helm, by Helm authors, with chart use cases in mind. They were placed into a separate library because they were generic enough that other applications could use them, too.

This is useful to know if you need functions for your Go-based application, find an issue in a function and want to report or fix it, or want to contribute a function of your own to Helm.

To illustrate functions we can look at a common pattern used in charts to improve readability. When helm create is run, as you saw in Chapter 4, a Kubernetes Deployment template is created as part of the chart. The Deployment template includes a section for a security context:

```
securityContext:
  {{- toYaml .Values.podSecurityContext | nindent 8 }}
```

Read the full chart from Chapter 4 at *https://github.com/Master minds/learning-helm/tree/main/chapter4/anvil*.

In the *values.yaml* file there is a YAML entry for podSecurityContext. This is meant to be the exact YAML passed in the template section of a Deployment for securityContext. Inside, the template the information from the *values.yaml* file is no longer YAML. Instead it is a data object. The toYaml function turns the data into YAML.

The YAML under securityContext needs to be indented properly or the Deployment's manifest will have YAML errors due to a section not being properly indented. This is accomplished through the use of two functions. To the left of toYaml a - is used with {{ to remove all the whitespace up to the : on the previous line. The output of toYaml is passed to nindent. This function adds a newline at the start of the text it receives and then indents each line.

nindent is used instead of the indent function for readability. The indent function does not add a newline at the beginning. nindent is used so that the YAML under securityContext can be on a new line. This is another common pattern found in templates.

In addition to toYaml, Helm has functions to convert data to JSON with toJson and to TOML with toToml. toYaml is often used when creating Kubernetes manifests, while toJson and toToml are more often used when creating configuration files to be passed to applications through Secrets and ConfigMaps.

The order of arguments passed into a function is intentional. When pipelines are used, the output of one function is passed as the last argument to the next function in the pipeline. In the previous example the output of toYaml is passed as the last argument to nindent, which takes two arguments. The order of arguments on functions is designed for common pipeline use cases.

There are more than a hundred functions (*https://oreil.ly/Xtoya*) available to use within templates. These include functions for handling math, dictionaries and lists, reflection, hash generation, date functions, and much more.

Methods

Up to this point, you have seen template functions. Helm also includes functions that detect the capabilities of a Kubernetes cluster and methods to work with files.

The .Capabilities object has the method .Capabilities.APIVersions.Has, which takes in a single argument for the Kubernetes API or type you want to check the existence of. It returns either true or false to let you know if that resource is available in your cluster. You can check for a group and version such as batch/v1 or a resource type such as apps/v1/Deployment.

Checking for the existence of resources and API groups is useful when dealing with custom resource definitions and multiple versions of Kubernetes resource types. As Kubernetes API versions move from alpha, to beta, to released versions, you want to use the latest version of a resource type as alpha and beta are deprecated and removed from Kubernetes. If your application will be installed on a wide range of Kubernetes versions, it is useful to support API versions in all of those clusters.

When `helm template` is used, Helm will use a default set of API versions for a compliant Kubernetes cluster instead of interacting with your cluster to generate the known capabilities.

The other place you will find methods is on `.Files`. It includes the following methods to help you work with files:

`.Files.Get name`
Provides a means of getting the contents of the file as a string. `name`, in this case, is the name including filepath from the root of the chart.

`.Files.GetBytes`
Similar to `.Files.Get` but instead of returning a string, the file is returned as an array of bytes. In Go terms, this is a byte slice (i.e., `[]byte`).

`.Files.Glob`
Accepts a glob pattern and returns another `files` object containing only the files whose names match the pattern.

`.Files.AsConfig`
Takes a files group and returns it as flattened YAML suitable to include in the `data` section of a Kubernetes `ConfigMap` manifest. This is useful when paired with `.Files.Glob`.

`.Files.AsSecrets`
Similar to `.Files.AsConfig`. Instead of returning flattened YAML it returns the data in a format that can be included in the `data` section of a Kubernetes `Secret` manifest. It's Base64 encoded. This is useful when paired with `.Files.Glob`. For example, `{{ .Files.Glob("mysecrets/**").AsSecrets }}`.

`.Files.Lines`
Has an argument for a filename and returns the contents of the file as an array split by newlines (i.e., `\n`).

To illustrate the use of these, the following template is from an *example* chart. It reads all the files in the *config* subdirectory of a chart and embeds each one in a `Secret`:

```
apiVersion: v1
kind: Secret
metadata:
  name: {{ include "example.fullname" . }}
type: Opaque
data:
{{ (.Files.Glob "config/*").AsSecrets | indent 2 }}
```

As the following example output from Helm shows, each file can be found at its own key in the file:

```
apiVersion: v1
kind: Secret
metadata:
  name: myapp
type: Opaque
data:
  jetpack.ini: ZW5hYmxlZCA9IHRydWU=
  rocket.yaml: ZW5hYmxlZDogdHJ1ZQ==
```

Querying Kubernetes Resources In Charts

Helm contains a template function that enables you to look up resources in the Kubernetes cluster. The lookup template function is able to return either an individual object or a list of objects. This function returns an empty response when commands that do not interact with the cluster are executed.

The following example looks up a Deployment named *runner* in the *anvil* namespace and makes the metadata annotations available:

```
{{ (lookup "apps/v1" "Deployment" "anvil" "runner").metadata.annotations }}
```

There are four arguments passed into the lookup function:

API version
   This is the version of any object, whether included in Kubernetes or installed as part of an add-on. Examples of this look like "v1" and "apps/v1".

Kind of object
   This can be any resource type.

Namespace to look for the object in
   This can be left blank to look in all namespaces you have access to or for global resources such as Namespace.

Name of the resource you are looking for
   This can be left blank to return a list of resources instead of a specific one.

When a list of resources is returned, you will need to loop over the results to access the data on each of the individual objects. Where a lookup for an object returns a *dict*, a lookup for a list of objects returns a *list*. These are two different types Helm provides for use in templates.

When a list is returned, the objects are on the items property:

```
{{ (lookup "v1" "ConfigMap" "anvil" "").items }}
```

The items can be iterated over using a loop, which you will learn about later in the chapter. This example returns all the ConfigMaps in the *anvil* namespace, assuming you have access to the namespace.

You should be careful when using this function. For example, it will return different results when used as part of a dry run as opposed to when an upgrade is run. A dry run does not interact with a cluster, so this function will return no results. When an upgrade is run it will return results.

The results returned when installing or upgrading in various clusters can also be different. For example, in a development environment and in a production environment the resources installed in a cluster will have differences that can lead to unequal responses.

if/else/with

Go templates have if and else statements along with something similar but mildly different called with. if and else work the same way they do in most programming languages. To illustrate an if statement, we can look at a pattern from the chart generated using the helm create command covered in Chapter 4. In that chart the *values.yaml* file contains a section on ingress with an enabled property. It looks like:

```
ingress:
  enabled: false
```

In the *ingress.yaml* file that creates the Ingress resource for Kubernetes, the first and last lines are for the if statement that implements this:

```
{{- if .Values.ingress.enabled -}}
...
{{- end }}
```

In this case, the if statement evaluates whether the output of the pipeline following the if statement is true or false. If it's true, the content inside is evaluated. In order to know where the end of the block is, you need an end statement. This is important because indentation or more typical brackets could be part of the material you want rendered.

Using if statements is how the common *enabled* pattern is typically implemented.

if statements can have an else statement that is executed if the if statement evaluates to false. The following example prints a YAML comment to output when Ingress is not enabled:

```
{{- if .Values.ingress.enabled -}}
...
{{- else -}}
# Ingress not enabled
{{- end }}
```

Sometimes you will want to have multiple elements evaluated in an `if` statement by combining them with an `and` or an `or` statement. In templates this is a little different than you might be used to. Consider the following segment from a template:

```
{{- if and .Values.characters .Values.products -}}
...
{{- end }}
```

In this case `and` is implemented as a function with two arguments. That means `and` comes before either of the two items being used. The same idea applies to the use of `or`, which is also implemented as a function.

When one of the elements to be used with `and` or `or` is a function or pipeline, you can use parentheses. The following example has one of the arguments to `or` being an equal check:

```
{{- if or (eq .Values.character "Wile E. Coyote") .Values.products -}}
...
{{- end }}
```

The output of the equality check, implemented using the `eq` function, is passed as the first argument to `or`. The parentheses enable you to group elements together to build more complex logic.

`with` is similar to `if` with the caveat that the scope within a `with` block changes. To continue with an example from `Ingress`, the following block shows the scope change:

```
{{- with .Values.ingress.annotations }}
annotations:
  {{- toYaml . | nindent 4 }}
{{- end }}
```

If the value passed into `with` is empty, the block is skipped. If the value is not empty, the block is executed and the value of `.` inside the block is `.Values.ingress.annotations`. In this situation, the scope within the block has changed to the value checked by `with`.

> The pattern of checking a value using `with` and then sending it to output using the `toYaml` and `nindent` functions is common for elements you have in a *values.yaml* file that you want to directly output in a template. This is regularly used for image pull secrets, node selectors, and more.

Just like with `if` statements, `with` can have an accompanying `else` block that you can use when the value is empty.

Variables

Within templates you can create your own variables and use them to pass as arguments to functions, print in the output, and more. Variables start with a $ and are typed. Once a variable is created for one type, such as a string, you cannot set the value to another type, such as an integer.

Creating and initializing a variable has a special syntax through the use of :=, like the following example:

```
{{ $var := .Values.character }}
```

In this case a new variable is created and the value of .Values.character is assigned to it. This variable can be used elsewhere; for example:

```
character: {{ $var | default "Sylvester" | quote }}
```

The value of $var is passed to default in the same way .Values.character was passed earlier in the chapter.

The method to create a variable with an initial value is different from the method used to change the value of an existing variable. When you assign a new value to the existing variable, you use =. For example:

```
{{ $var := .Values.character }}
{{ $var = "Tweety" }}
```

In this case the variable is changed in another action. Variables live on for the life of the template execution and are available in the same action or different ones later in the template.

> Variable handling is reflective of the syntax and style used in the Go programming language. It follows the same semantics through the use of :=, =, and typing.

Loops

Using loops is a common method to simplify a user's interaction with a chart. For example, you can use loops to collect a list of hosts to use when exposing a web application, through values, and then loop over the list to create more complex Kubernetes Ingress resources.

The loop syntax in templates is a little different than that in many programming languages. Instead of for loops, there are range loops that can be used to iterate over *dicts* (also known as maps) and lists.

The following example illustrates dicts and lists:

```
# An example list in YAML
characters:
  - Sylvester
  - Tweety
  - Road Runner
  - Wile E. Coyote

# An example map in YAML
products:
  anvil: They ring like a bell
  grease: 50% slippery
  boomerang: Guaranteed to return
```

You can think of a list as an array, while a map, with a key name and value, is similar to dictionaries in Python or a HashMap in Java. Within Helm templates you can create your own dictionaries and lists using the dict and list functions.

There are two ways you can use the range function. The following example iterates over the *characters* while changing the scope, which is the value of .:

```
characters:
{{- range .Values.characters }}
  - {{ . | quote }}
{{- end }}
```

In this case range iterates over each item in the list and sets the value of . to the value of each item in the list as Helm iterates over the item. In this example, the value is passed to quote in the pipeline. The scope for . is changed in the block up to end, which acts as the closing bracket or statement for the loop.

The output of this snippet is:

```
characters:
  - "Sylvester"
  - "Tweety"
  - "Road Runner"
  - "Wile E. Coyote"
```

The other way to use range is by having it create new variables for the key and value. This will work on both lists and dicts. This next example creates the variables that you can use in the block:

```
products:
{{- range $key, $value := .Values.products }}
  - {{ $key }}: {{ $value | quote }}
{{- end }}
```

The $key variable contains the key in a map or dict and a number in a list. $value contains the value. If this is a complex type, such as another dict, that will be available as the $value. The new variables are in scope up to the end of the range block, which is signified by the corresponding end action. The output of this example is:

```
products:
  - anvil: "They ring like a bell"
  - boomerang: "Guaranteed to return"
  - grease: "50% slippery"
```

Under the Hood: dict and list

Within Go, lists are represented as slices that are backed by arrays. The value is an interface, so it could be a variety of types. For example, if you use the list function to create a list within a template the returned value would be typed as []interface{}. When actions are taken on the value, reflection is used to figure out the type and how to act on that type.

A map or dict is represented a little differently. They are typically represented as map[*string*]interface{}. This is the type returned from the dict function that you can use within templates. As with lists, the value type is figured out using reflection when action is taken on the value.

Named Templates

There are times where you will want to create a template to call from within your template of a Kubernetes manifest—for example, when you have a value generated by some complex logic or when you have a section that is repeated across numerous Kubernetes manifests. You can create your own templates, which Helm won't automatically render, and use them within templates of Kubernetes manifests.

An example of this can be found when you run helm create to generate a chart. By default Helm creates several Kubernetes manifests with some shared elements, such as labels. To keep the labels consistent and so they only need to be updated in one place, Helm generates a template and then calls that template each time the labels are needed.

There are two types of labels used in the templates. There are the labels used on higher-level resources, such as Deployments, and then there are the labels used in specifications that are paired with selectors used for updates. These labels need to be treated differently because the labels used on specifications and selectors are typically immutable. This means you won't want them to contain elements such as application versions because those can change as an application is upgraded, but the specifications and selectors cannot be updated with new versions.

The following template selection contains the selector labels used to generate specifications and selector sections in the generated template. The name, *anvil*, is from the
chart generated in Chapter 4:

```
{{/*
Selector labels ❶
*/}}
{{- define "anvil.selectorLabels" -}} ❷
app.kubernetes.io/name: {{ include "anvil.name" . }} ❸
app.kubernetes.io/instance: {{ .Release.Name }}
{{- end -}} ❹
```

❶ A comment prior to defining the function. Comments in actions open with /*
and are closed by */.

❷ You define a template with a `define` statement followed by the name for the template.

❸ The content of a template is just like the content of any other template.

❹ The definition for a template is closed through an `end` statement that matches to
the `define` statement.

This template includes several useful things you should consider using in your own
templates:

1. A comment describing the template. This is ignored when the template is rendered but is useful in the same way code comments are.

2. The name is namespaced, using . as the separator, to include the chart name. In
Chapter 6 you will learn about library charts and dependent charts. Using a
namespace on a template name enables the use of library charts and avoids colli-
sions on dependent charts.

3. The `define` and `end` calls use actions that remove whitespace before and after
them so that their use does not add extra lines to the final output YAML.

This template is called in the `spec` section of resources, such as the `Deployment` in the
anvil chart:

```
spec:
  replicas: {{ .Values.replicaCount }}
  selector:
    matchLabels:
      {{- include "anvil.selectorLabels" . | nindent 6 }}
  template:
    metadata:
      labels:
        {{- include "anvil.selectorLabels" . | nindent 8 }}
```

The `matchLabels` section here is immutable, so it cannot be changed and it looks for the `labels` in the `template` section.

There are two functions you can use to include another template in your template. The `template` function is a basic function for including another template. It cannot be used in pipelines. Then there is the `include` function that works in a similar manner but can be used in pipelines. In the preceding example, `include` is used to call another template and the output of that template is passed to `nindent` to ensure the output has the proper indentation level. Since the output has a different indentation level for each call, the indentation level cannot be included as part of the template that defines it.

The `include` function takes two arguments. The first is the name of the template to call. This needs to be the full name including any namespace. The second is the data object to pass. This can be one you create yourself, using the `dict` function, or it can be all or part of the global object used within the template. In this case the whole global object is passed in.

The template function Helm created to generate the wider selection of labels, used on the labels for the higher-level resources where the labels are mutable, both adds labels and includes the selector labels. It has user-defined templates that call other user-defined templates:

```
{{/*
Common labels
*/}}
{{- define "anvil.labels" -}}
helm.sh/chart: {{ include "anvil.chart" . }}
{{ include "anvil.selectorLabels" . }}
{{- if .Chart.AppVersion }}
app.kubernetes.io/version: {{ .Chart.AppVersion | quote }}
{{- end }}
app.kubernetes.io/managed-by: {{ .Release.Service }}
{{- end -}}
```

Because these labels are mutable, there are useful labels included here that will change for various reasons. So as not to repeat the labels used for selectors, which are useful here as well, those labels are included by calling the function that generates them.

Kubernetes Recommended Labels

The Kubernetes documentation recommends a set of common labels that you can apply to your workload manifests. The chart generated by `helm create` includes templates that generate these labels for you.

The labels begin with the prefix *app.kubernetes.io* followed by / as a separator. The Kubernetes documentation for labels notes that a prefix should be used for any labels generated by automation and that those without a prefix are private to the user. These labels are for users, like you, and for various tools.

These labels include the application's name, the instance of the application (you can run an application more than once in a cluster and even a single namespace), the version of the application, a component type used to show where it fits in a larger application, what the application is part of, and the name of the tool used to manage the life cycle of the application (e.g., Helm). These labels are useful when linking applications together, displaying metadata in a user interface, and querying for information at the Kubernetes API.

You can learn more about the labels, which includes examples, in the Kubernetes documentation (*https://oreil.ly/uAFIm*).

Another situation you may find yourself in where a named template would be useful is when you want to encapsulate complex logic. To illustrate this idea, consider a chart where you want to be able to pass in a container version as a tag, a digest, or fall back on the application version as a default. The part of the Pod specification that accepts the container image, including the version, is a single line. To provide all three of those options you need many lines of logic:

```
{{- define "anvil.getImage" -}}
{{- if .Values.image.digest -}}
{{ .Values.image.repository }}@{{ .Values.image.digest }}
{{- else -}}
{{ .Values.image.repository }}:
{{- .Values.image.tag | default .Chart.AppVersion }}
{{- end -}}
{{- end -}}
```

This new getImage template is able to handle a digest, tag, and default to the application version if neither of the other two are present. First, a digest is checked for and used. A digest is immutable, and it is the most precise method to specify the revision of an image to use. If no digest is passed in, a tag is checked. Tags are pointers to digests and can be changed. If no tag is found, the AppVersion is used as a tag.

This function targets the structure of the *anvil* chart, first created for Chapter 4. The image details are expected to be within the structure of that chart and its *values.yaml* file.

In the template for the Deployment, the image would be referenced using the new function:

```
image: "{{ include "anvil.getImage" . }}"
```

Templates can act like functions in a software program. They are a useful way for you to break off complex logic and have shared functionality.

Structuring Your Templates for Maintainability

There is limited structure that is enforced on the templates in the *templates* directory. Multiple Kubernetes manifests can be in the same YAML file, which means that the templates for multiple Kubernetes manifests can be in the same file, too. Named templates can live in any of the template files and be referenced in the others. The *NOTES.txt* template is a special file that displays to the user, and tests are handled in a special way. Tests are covered in Chapter 6. Other than that, it is a blank canvas for you to create templates.

To aid in creating maintainable templates that are easy to navigate, the Helm maintainers recommend several patterns. These patterns are useful for a few reasons:

- You may go long periods without making structural changes to the templates in a chart and then come back to it. Being able to quickly rediscover the layout will make the processes faster.

- Other people will look at the templates in charts. This may be team members who create the chart or those that consume it. Consumers can, and sometimes do, open up a chart to inspect it prior to installing it or as part of a process to fork it.

- When you debug a chart, which is covered in the next section, it is easier to do so with some structure in the templates.

The first pattern is that each Kubernetes manifest should be in its own template file and that file should have a descriptive name. For example, name your template *deployment.yaml* if there is a single deployment. If you have the case of multiple manifests of the same type, such as the case when you have a database deployed using primaries and replicas, you use names such as *statefulset-primary.yaml* and *statefulset-replica.yaml*.

A second guideline is to put the named templates, which you include in your own templates, into a file named *_helpers.tpl*. Because these are essentially helper templates for your other templates, the name is descriptive. As mentioned earlier, the _ at the start of the name causes it to bubble up to the top of directory listings so you can easily find it among your templates.

When you use the `helm create` command to start a new chart, the contents of the templates it starts with, by default, will already follow these patterns.

Debugging Templates

When developing templates it's useful to debug the templates. Helm provides three features you can use in your development workflow to find issues. These are in addition to testing, which is covered in Chapter 6.

Dry Run

The commands to install, upgrade, roll back, and uninstall Helm charts all have a flag to initiate a dry run and simulate the process but not fully execute on that process. This is accomplished using the --dry-run flag on these commands. For example, if you use the --dry-run flag on the install command on the *anvil* chart, you could use the command helm install myanvil anvil --dry-run. Helm would render the templates, check the templates to make sure what would be sent to Kubernetes was well formed, and would then send it to output. The output would look similar to the output on a normal install but would have two additional sections:

```
NAME: myanvil
LAST DEPLOYED: Tue Jun  9 06:58:58 2020
NAMESPACE: default
STATUS: pending-install
REVISION: 1
HOOKS:
...
MANIFEST:
...
NOTES:
1. Get the application URL by running these commands:
   export POD_NAME=$(kubectl get pods --namespace default ↵
     -l "app.kubernetes.io/name=anvil,app.kubernetes.io/instance=myanvil" ↵
     -o jsonpath="{.items[0].metadata.name}")
   echo "Visit http://127.0.0.1:8080 to use your application"
   kubectl --namespace default port-forward $POD_NAME 8080:80
```

The two new sections are the *HOOKS* and *MANIFEST* sections that will contain the YAML Helm would normally pass to Kubernetes. Instead it is sent to the output. For brevity the full generated YAML is not included because this would be pages long.

If there were a problem in the templates, the response would be quite different. To illustrate this, try removing the first } from the *deployment.yaml* file in the *anvil* chart and performing a dry-run install again. Removing the } will cause an error parsing the actions in the templates. Instead of outputting the status, Helm will output an error like:

```
Error: parse error at (anvil/templates/deployment.yaml:4): unexpected "}" in
operand
```

The information here outlines a hint where to look for the issue. It includes:

- The file where the error is occurring. *anvil/templates/deployment.yaml*, in this case.

- The line number in the file where the error occurred. Here it is line 4.

- An error message with a hint about the problem. The error message will often not display what the issue is, but rather where the parser is having an issue. In this case a single } is unexpected.

Helm will check for more than errors in the template syntax. It will also check the syntax of the output. To illustrate this, in the same *deployment.yaml* file remove the `apiVersion:` at the start of it. Make sure to add back the missing } so that the action is fixed. The beginning of the file will now look like:

```
apps/v1
kind: Deployment
```

Performing a dry-run install will produce the following output:

```
Error: YAML parse error on anvil/templates/deployment.yaml: error converting
YAML to JSON: yaml: line 2: mapping values are not allowed in this context
```

You might be wondering why there is an error converting between YAML and JSON. This is a product of the YAML parsing library that Helm and Kubernetes use. The useful part of the error message is the part that starts with `line 2`. The first line is not complete, so the second line is in the wrong context even though it is well formed. The file is not valid YAML, and Helm is telling you where to start looking for the problem. If you took the same section of YAML and tested it in an online YAML validator, you would get the same error.

Helm is also able to validate the schemas of Kubernetes resources. This is accomplished because Kubernetes provides schema definitions for its manifests. To illustrate this, change the `apiVersion` in the *deployment.yaml* to be `foo`:

```
foo: apps/v1
kind: Deployment
```

Performing a dry-run install will produce the following output:

```
Error: unable to build kubernetes objects from release manifest: error
validating "": error validating data: apiVersion not set
```

The deployment is no longer valid, and Helm was able to provide specific feedback on what is missing. In this case, the `apiVersion` property is not set.

Utilizing a dry-run isn't the only way you can get access to this feature. The `helm template` command provides a similar experience but without the full debugging feature set. The `template` command does turn the `template` commands into YAML. At this point it will provide an error if the generated YAML cannot be parsed. What it won't do is validate the YAML against the Kubernetes schema. The `template` command won't warn you if `apiVersion` is turned to `foo`. This is due to Helm not communicating with a Kubernetes cluster to get the schema for validation when the `template` command is used.

Getting Installed Manifests

There are times where you install an application into a cluster and something else changes the manifests afterwards. This leads to differences between what you declared and what you have running. One example of this is when a service mesh automatically adds a sidecar container to the Pods created by your Helm charts.

Service Mesh

A service mesh is a layer of infrastructure used to manage service-to-service communications. In Kubernetes, a service mesh uses a sidecar proxy container added to Pods to handle the communication. Many service mesh platforms offer the ability to automatically inject the sidecar proxies by altering the configuration of manifests.

You can get the original manifests deployed by Helm using the `helm get manifest` command. This command will retrieve the manifests for a release as they were when Helm installed the release. It is able to retrieve this information for any revision of a release still available in the history, as found using the `helm history` command.

To continue the *myanvil* example, to retrieve the manifests for this instance of the *anvil* chart you would run:

```
$ helm get manifest myanvil
```

The output will include all of the manifests with `---` at the start of each new manifest. The following is the first 15 lines from the output:

```
---
# Source: anvil/templates/serviceaccount.yaml
apiVersion: v1
kind: ServiceAccount
metadata:
  name: myanvil-anvil
  labels:
    helm.sh/chart: anvil-0.1.0
    app.kubernetes.io/name: anvil
    app.kubernetes.io/instance: myanvil
    app.kubernetes.io/version: "9.17.49"
    app.kubernetes.io/managed-by: Helm
---
# Source: anvil/templates/service.yaml
apiVersion: v1
kind: Service
...
```

`---` is used as a separator between YAML documents. In addition to that, Helm adds a YAML comment with the source template used to generate the manifest.

Linting Charts

Some of the problems you will encounter don't show up as violations of the API specification and aren't problems in the templates. For example, Kubernetes resources are required to have names that can be used as part of a domain name. This restricts the characters that you can use in names and their length. The OpenAPI schema provided by Kubernetes does not provide enough information to detect names that will fail when sent to Kubernetes. The *lint* command, previously covered in Chapter 4, is able to detect problems like this and tell you where they are.

To illustrate this you can modify the *anvil* chart to add Wile to the end of the Deployment name in *deployment.yaml*:

```
apiVersion: apps/v1
kind: Deployment
metadata:
  name: {{ include "anvil.fullname" . }}-Wile
```

Running helm lint anvil will produce an error informing you of the issue:

```
$ helm lint anvil
==> Linting anvil
[ERROR] templates/deployment.yaml: object name does not conform to Kubernetes
naming requirements: "test-release-anvil-Wile"

Error: 1 chart(s) linted, 1 chart(s) failed
```

In this case, helm lint is pointing you to a problem and telling you where it is happening.

Conclusion

The templates you include in a chart provide a powerful ability to create resources within Kubernetes. It's akin to a programming language around templates. The template system has features like logic, built-in functions, custom templates, and debugging. This means you can collect the input you desire through values and generate the Kubernetes manifests you need.

There is still more to charts, including dependencies, testing, schemas for values files, and more. Chapter 6 is going to expand on what you can have and do with charts.

Advanced Chart Features

There is more to charts than metadata about the chart and a collection of templates. Charts can have dependencies, values can have schemas, Helm has life cycle hooks, you can sign charts, and more. In this chapter you will learn about other elements of charts, moving beyond templates.

These features provide powerful solutions to common problems that arise when building packages. The chapter starts by covering dependencies. Dependencies are a critical part of virtually every package management solution because they let you leverage existing packages in your solution and build on the work of others. It then goes on to cover schemas and validation, which are useful when you want to help chart users avoid issues before covering ways you can hook into processes Helm performs to execute custom actions. This chapter covers tests and testing as well—tests are vital in development because they ensure your software is running as expected. Helm provides security features that aid in mitigating some common threat paths, which are covered next. The chapter concludes by looking at how charts can be used to extend the Kubernetes API.

Throughout this chapter, you will see charts as examples you can reference at *https:// github.com/masterminds/learning-helm/blob/main/chapter6*. They showcase different features covered in the chapter along with a Helm repository.

Chart Dependencies

Dependencies are a common element of package managers and their packages. Charts can have dependencies on other charts. This enables the encapsulation of a service in a chart, the reuse of charts, and the use of multiple charts together.

To illustrate dependencies, consider a chart to install WordPress, the popular blogging software. WordPress depends on a MySQL-compliant database to store the blog content, users, and other configuration. A MySQL-compliant database can be used by other applications and can be consumed as a service. One way to handle the use of MySQL with WordPress is to put the manifests for it in the WordPress chart. Another way to handle it is to have a MySQL chart that stands alone while the WordPress chart has a dependency on it. Having a MySQL-compliant database as an independent chart enables it to be used by more than one application, and the database can be built and tested independently.

Dependencies are specified in the *Chart.yaml* file. The following is the `dependencies` section in the *Chart.yaml* file for a chart named *rocket*:

```
dependencies:
  - name: booster ❶
    version: ^1.0.0 ❷
    repository: https://raw.githubusercontent.com/Masterminds/learning-helm/main/
      chapter6/repository/ ❸
```

❶ The name of the dependent chart within the repository.

❷ A version range string for the chart.

❸ The repository to retrieve the chart from.

Helm charts use semantic versions as their versioning scheme. The `version` field used for dependencies accepts a version range, and there are some shorthand syntaxes for those ranges. For example, `^1.2.3` is shorthand for `>= 1.2.3, < 2.0.0`. Helm supports ranges including =, !=, <, ⇐, >, >=, ^, ~, and -. Different ranges can be combined together using a space or comma to support logical *and* combinations and | to support logical *or* combinations. Helm also supports using a wildcard character of either X or *. If you omit a section of a version, such as omitting the patch portion, Helm will assume the missing part is a wildcard.

Ranges are the preferred manner to specify the desired version. In a moment you'll learn how to lock to a specific dependency version from the specified range. By specifying a range, it is possible to use Helm commands to automatically update to the latest release within that range. This is useful if you want to pull in bug fixes or security updates to dependencies.

Shorthand Range Syntaxes

While semantic versions are defined from a specification, the range syntaxes in use to specify semantic version ranges have no specification. Different tools will use different algorithms for the same shorthand syntaxes of ^ and ~. Helm follows the same syntax used by JavaScript with npm and Rust with Cargo.

For major versions greater than 0, when you use ^ it does a range that is greater than or equal to the number you set and less than the next major version. When the major version is less than 1, Helm typically treats the minor version as the range it works in instead of the major version. The following are examples of the ranges and equivalent meanings:

- `^1.2.3` is equivalent to `>= 1.2.3 < 2.0.0`
- `^1.2.x` is equivalent to `>= 1.2.0 < 2.0.0`
- `^2.3` is equivalent to `>= 2.3 < 3`
- `^2.x` is equivalent to `>= 2.0.0 < 3`
- `^0.2.3` is equivalent to `>= 0.2.3 < 0.3.0`
- `^0.2` is equivalent to `>= 0.2.0 < 0.3.0`
- `^0.0.3` is equivalent to `>= 0.0.3 < 0.0.4`
- `^0.0` is equivalent to `>= 0.0.0 < 0.1.0`
- `^0` is equivalent to `>= 0.0.0 < 1.0.0`

~ is used for specifying patch ranges. Where ^ typically rounds up to the latest within a major version range, ~ rounds up within a minor version range as long as the minor version is specified. The following examples illustrate ~:

- `~1.2.3` is equivalent to `>= 1.2.3 < 1.3.0`
- `~1` is equivalent to `>= 1 < 2`
- `~2.3` is equivalent to `>= 2.3 < 2.4`
- `~1.2.x` is equivalent to `>= 1.2.0 < 1.3.0`
- `~1.x` is equivalent to `>= 1 < 2`

The `repository` field is where you specify the chart repository location to pull the dependency from. You can specify this in one of the following two ways:

- A URL to the Helm repository.
- To the name of a repository you have set up using the `helm repo add` command. This name needs to be preceded by an @ and wrapped in quotes (e.g., `"@myrepo"`).

A full URL is typically used to specify the location. This will ensure the same dependency is retrieved in every environment the chart is used in.

Once you have the dependencies with their requested version ranges specified, you need to use Helm to lock those dependencies to specific versions and retrieve the dependencies. If you are going to package up your chart as a chart archive as covered in Chapter 4, you need to lock and fetch dependencies before packaging.

To resolve the latest version of the dependency within the specified range and to retrieve it, you can use the following command:

```
$ helm dependency update .
```

After running the command you will see the following output:

```
Saving 1 charts
Downloading booster from repo https://raw.githubusercontent.com/Masterminds/
  learning-helm/main/chapter6/repository/
Deleting outdated charts
```

Running this command caused a few steps to happen.

First, Helm resolved the latest version of the *booster* chart. It used the metadata in the repository to know which versions of the chart were available. From the metadata and the specified version range, Helm found the best match.

The resolved information is written to the *Chart.lock* file. Instead of a version range, the *Chart.lock* file contains the specific version of the dependencies to be used. This is important for reproducibility. The *Chart.lock* file is managed by Helm. Changes from users will be overwritten the next time `helm dep up` (the shorthand syntax) is run. This is similar to lock files for dependency managers on other platforms.

Once Helm knows the specific version to use, it downloads the dependent chart and puts it into the *charts* subdirectory. It is important for the dependent charts to be in the *charts* directory because this is where Helm will get their contents from to render the templates. Charts can be in the *charts* directory in either their archive or directory form. When Helm downloads them from a repository, it stores them in their archive form.

If you have a *Chart.lock* file but no contents in the *charts* directory, you can rebuild the *charts* directory by running the command `helm dependency build`. This will use the lock file to retrieve the dependencies at their already determined versions.

Once you have dependencies, Helm will render their resources when you run commands like `helm install` or `helm upgrade`.

When you specify a dependency, you may also want to pass configuration from the parent or main chart to the dependent chart. If we look back at the WordPress example, this could be used to set the name of the database to use. Helm provides a method to do this within the parent chart's values.

In the main chart's *values.yaml* file, you can create a new section with the name of the dependent chart. In this section you can set the values you want passed in. You only need to set the ones you want changed because the dependent charts included in the *values.yaml* file will serve as the default values.

In the *values.yaml* file for the *rocket* chart there is a section that reads:

```
booster:
  image:
    tag: 9.17.49
```

Helm knows this section is for the *booster* chart. In this case it sets the image tag to a specific value. Any of the values in the dependent chart can be set this way. When commands like `helm install` are run, you can use the flags to set values (e.g., `--set`) of the dependencies as well as those of the main chart.

If you have two dependencies on the same chart you can optionally use the `alias` property in the *Chart.yaml* file. This property goes on each dependency you want to use an alternative name for next to the `name`, `version`, and other properties. With `alias` you can give each dependency a unique name that you can reference elsewhere, such as in the *values.yaml* file.

Tightly Versus Loosely Coupled Dependencies

When you have dependencies, you can tightly couple or loosely couple them. Using the *Chart.yaml* file to specify dependencies causes a tight coupling between charts. You can see this in the way upgrades work. To upgrade one chart you must upgrade the whole group. There are benefits to tight coupling, such as a single Helm command being able to install the whole collection of charts. A tight coupling is useful when you want to distribute charts to others, outside your company or organization.

In a loose coupling situation you can install each chart independently from the rest. Each chart will run as its own instance. In this setup, each instance acts as a service that other services can connect to. With a loose coupling you can change and upgrade each chart independently from the rest. This method is sometimes used when you create and run charts within your own organization.

Conditional Flags for Enabling Dependencies

Helm provides the ability for you to enable or disable dependencies through configuration. To illustrate this idea, consider the case where you want to provide a WordPress blogging solution but give the option to the personnel installing WordPress to either use a database as a service or an included database. If the person installing the chart chooses to use a database as a service, they would provide a URL to that service and not need to have a database installed. This can be accomplished through configuration in two different ways.

When you want to control if a single feature is enabled or disabled through a dependency, you can use the `condition` property on a dependency. To illustrate this we will look at the `dependencies` section in the *Chart.yaml* file for the conditional chart:

```
dependencies:
  - name: booster
    version: ^1.0.0
    condition: booster.enabled
    repository: https://raw.githubusercontent.com/Masterminds/learning-helm/main/
      chapter6/repository/
```

The dependency has a `condition` key with a value that tells Helm where to look in the values to know if it should be enabled or disabled. In the *values.yaml* file the corresponding section is:

```
booster:
  enabled: false
```

The default value, in this case, is to disable the dependency. When someone installs the chart they can enable the dependency by passing in a value to enable it.

When you have multiple features you want to enable or disable that involve dependencies, you can use the `tags` property. Like `condition`, this property sits alongside the `name` and `version` when describing a dependency. It contains a list of tags for a dependency. To illustrate this we can look at the dependencies of another chart named *tag*:

```
dependencies:
  - name: booster
    tags:
      - faster
    version: ^1.0.0
    repository: https://raw.githubusercontent.com/Masterminds/learning-helm/main/
      chapter6/repository/
  - name: rocket
    tags:
      - faster
    version: ^1.0.0
    repository: https://raw.githubusercontent.com/Masterminds/learning-helm/main/
      chapter6/repository/
```

Here you will see two dependencies with a `tags` section. The tags are a list of related tags. In the chart's *values.yaml* file you use a `tags` property:

```
tags:
  faster: false
```

`tags` is a property with a special meaning. The values here tell Helm to disable dependencies with the tag *faster* by default. They can be enabled when the chart's user passes a true value into the chart as it's being installed or upgraded.

Importing Values from Child to Parent Charts

There are times where you may want to import or pull values from a child to a parent chart. Helm provides two methods to do this. One is for the case where a child chart explicitly exported a value to be imported by a parent, and the other is for the case in which the child chart did not export a value.

The exports property

The `exports` property is a special top-level property in a *values.yaml* file. When a child chart has declared an `export` property, its contents can be imported directly into a parent chart.

For example, consider the following from a child chart's *values.yaml* file:

```
exports:
  types:
    foghorn: rooster
```

When the parent chart declares the child as a dependency, it can import from the exports like the following:

```
dependencies:
  - name: example-child
    version: ^1.0.0
    repository: https://charts.example.com/
    import-values:
      - types
```

Within the parent's calculated values the types are now accessible at the top level. In YAML that would be equivalent to:

```
foghorn: rooster
```

The child-parent format

When a parent chart wants to import a value from a child but the child chart hasn't exported the value, there is a way to tell Helm to pull the child value into the parent chart.

To illustrate this, consider a child chart with the following values specified in its *values.yaml* file:

```
types:
  foghorn: rooster
```

These values are not exported, but the parent chart can import them anyway. When the dependency is declared in the parent, it can import the values using `child` and `parent` files, like the following example:

```
dependencies:
  - name: example-child
```

```
version: ^1.0.0
repository: https://charts.example.com/
import-values:
  - child: types
    parent: characters
```

In both methods of importing it's the `import-values` property that's used on the dependency. Helm knows how to differentiate between the different formats, and you can mix the two.

In the child chart the top-level property of `types` will not be available in the parent chart under the top-level property of `characters` in its calculated values. That would be represented in YAML as:

```
characters:
  foghorn: rooster
```

This format does allow for accessing nested values in addition to top-level properties using a period as a separator. For example, if the child chart had the following format, the `child` property on `import-values` could read `data.types`:

```
data:
  types:
    foghorn: rooster
```

Library Charts

You may run into the situation where you are creating multiple similar charts—charts that share a lot of the same templates. For these situations, there are library charts.

Library charts are conceptually similar to software libraries. They provide reusable functionality that can be imported and used by other charts but cannot be installed themselves.

If you use `helm create` to create a new library chart, the first step is to remove the contents of the *templates* directory and the *values.yaml* file because neither of these will be used. Then, you need to tell Helm that this is a library chart. In the *Chart.yaml* file set the `type` to `library`. To illustrate this, here is the *Chart.yaml* file from a chart named *mylib*:

```
apiVersion: v2
name: mylib
type: library
description: an example library chart
version: 0.1.0
```

The default value for `type`, when not set, is application. You only need to set it when your chart is a library.

Files in the *templates* directory that start with an underscore (i.e., _) are not expected to render manifests to send to Kubernetes. The convention is that helper templates and snippets are in _*.tpl and _*.yaml files.

To illustrate how reusable templates work, the following is the template to create a ConfigMap in the *mylib* chart file named *_configmap.yaml*:

```
{{- define "mylib.configmap.tpl" -}}
apiVersion: v1
kind: ConfigMap
metadata:
  name: {{ include "mylib.fullname" . }} ❶
  labels:
    {{- include "mylib.labels" . | nindent 4 }} ❷
data: {}
{{- end -}}
{{- define "mylib.configmap" -}} ❸
{{- template "mylib.util.merge" (append . "mylib.configmap.tpl") -}}
{{- end -}}
```

❶   The fullname function is the same as the one generated by helm create.

❷   The labels function generates the common labels Helm recommends to use in charts.

❸   A special template is defined that knows how to merge templates together.

Most of this definition looks similar to other templates you would put into the *templates* directory. define is a function used to define a template that is used elsewhere. There are two templates defined in this file. *mylib.configmap.tpl* contains a template for a resource. This will look similar to other templates. It provides a blueprint that is meant to be overridden by the caller in a chart that includes this library. *mylib.configmap* is a special template. This is the template another chart will use. It takes *mylib.configmap.tpl* along with another template, yet to be defined, containing overrides, and merges them into one output. *mylib.configmap* uses a utility function that handles the merging and is handy to reuse. That function is:

```
{{- /*
mylib.util.merge will merge two YAML templates and output the result.
This takes an array of three values:
- the top context
- the template name of the overrides (destination)
- the template name of the base (source)
*/ -}}
{{- define "mylib.util.merge" -}}
{{- $top := first . -}}
{{- $overrides := fromYaml (include (index . 1) $top) | default (dict ) -}}
{{- $tpl := fromYaml (include (index . 2) $top) | default (dict ) -}}
```

```
{{- toYaml (merge $overrides $tpl) -}}
{{- end -}}
```

This function takes a context (think about the . data covered in Chapter 5), a template containing overrides, and the base template function to be overridden. The function will become more clear when you see how it is used.

 The concept of library charts was developed prior to their official inclusion in Helm. The merge function was created by Adnan Abdulhussein as part of his work developing the idea through a chart named *Common*.

To illustrate using this library function, the following template is from another chart named *mychart*. Prior to using the resources it defines, it needs to be added as a dependency, just like any other. A template is included in *mychart* to create a Config Map:

```
{{- include "mylib.configmap" (list . "mychart.configmap") -}} ❶
{{- define "mychart.configmap" -}} ❷
data: ❸
  myvalue: "Hello Bosko"
{{- end -}}
```

❶ Including and using the function from the library chart for the ConfigMap.

❷ A new template is defined with just the parts to override the template provided by the library.

❸ The data section is provided for use in the ConfigMap.

This template may appear to be confusing at first because there is a lot going on.

The first line includes the ConfigMap template from the library chart. A new list is passed to it with two items. The first is the current data object, and the second is the name of another template containing elements to override those provided by the library chart.

The rest of the file is the template containing overrides. In the template provided by the library chart no content was provided for the data section. It is empty. The function mychart.configmap provides a data section.

The Helm rendered output from this template is:

```
apiVersion: v1
kind: ConfigMap
metadata:
  labels:
    app.kubernetes.io/instance: example
```

```
      app.kubernetes.io/managed-by: Helm
      app.kubernetes.io/name: mychart
      helm.sh/chart: mychart-0.1.0
   name: example-mychart
data:
   myvalue: Hello Bosko
```

This output is the merged output from the library and the chart consuming the
library. The same concept can be extended to other resources including those that are
longer and more complex.

Schematizing Values Files

The values defined by a *values.yaml* file are schemaless. There is no set structure that
all *values.yaml* files need to follow. Different charts have different structures. This
enables you to structure the values to the application or workload you're deploying
with the chart.

Schemas provide numerous useful benefits including the ability to validate content,
and you can do things such as generate user interfaces from them.

Helm provides the optional ability for each chart to provide its own schema for its
values using JSON Schema (*https://json-schema.org*). JSON Schema provides a
vocabulary to describe JSON files. YAML is a superset of JSON, and you can transform content between the two file formats. This makes it possible to use a JSON
Schema to validate the content of a YAML file.

When you run the commands `helm install`, `helm upgrade`, `helm lint`, and `helm
template`, Helm will validate the values against what it finds in the *values.schema.json*
file. The values Helm validates are the computed values. They include the values provided by the chart as well as the values passed in by the person installing the chart.
The *values.schema.json* file lives next to the *values.yaml* file in the root of a chart. The
file can describe all or part of the values.

Consider the following section from a *values.yaml* file:

```
image:
  repository: ghcr.io/masterminds/learning-helm/anvil-app
  pullPolicy: IfNotPresent
  tag: ""
```

A JSON Schema to check this would be:

```
{
    "$schema": "http://json-schema.org/schema#",
    "type": "object",
    "properties": {
        "image": {
            "type": "object", ❶
            "properties": {
```

```
                    "pullPolicy": {
                        "type": "string", ❷
                        "enum": ["Always", "IfNotPresent"] ❸
                    },
                    "repository": {
                        "type": "string"
                    },
                    "tag": {
                        "type": "string"
                    }
                }
            }
        }
    }
```

❶ image is an object. If image is passed to Helm as something other than an object, an error will be thrown.

❷ pullPolicy is a string. When other types, such as an integer, are passed in, an error will be thrown. This can catch subtle problems.

❸ The pullPolicy must be one of the listed values. When another value, even a misspelling, is passed in to Helm, an error will be thrown.

To illustrate this, we can use the *booster* chart. If you run the command from the root of the chart, you'll see an error:

```
$ helm lint . --set image.pullPolicy=foo
```

The following error tells you where the values don't match the schema:

```
==> Linting .
[ERROR] templates/: values don't meet the specifications of the schema(s) in the
following chart(s):
booster:
- image.pullPolicy: image.pullPolicy must be one of the following: "Always",
  "IfNotPresent"


Error: 1 chart(s) linted, 1 chart(s) failed
```

JSON Schemas provide several ways to describe properties. The most flexible method (a catch-all) is the use of regular expressions for strings. For example, instead of an enum a pattern of ^(Always|IfNotPresent)$ could have been used. The pattern would not have been as descriptive. The error would have noted the value didn't fit the pattern. Patterns are great to use when there is no other method to describe a property's value.

Schemas are a useful addition to charts that can catch and correct subtle issues someone may have when installing a chart.

Hooks

Helm provides a means to hook into events in the release process and take action. This is useful if you want to bundle actions as part of a release—for example, building in the ability to back up a database as part of the upgrade process while ensuring that the backup occurs prior to upgrading the Kubernetes resources.

Hooks are like regular templates and the functionality they encapsulate is provided through containers running in Kubernetes clusters alongside the other resources for your application. What distinguishes hooks from other resources is when a special annotation is set. When Helm sees the `helm.sh/hook` annotation, it uses the resource as a hook instead of a resource to be installed as part of the application installed by the chart. Table 6-1 contains a list of hooks and when they are executed.

Table 6-1. Helm hooks

Annotation value	Description
pre-install	Execution happens after resources are rendered but prior to those resources being uploaded to Kubernetes.
post-install	Execution happens after resources have been uploaded to Kubernetes.
pre-delete	Execution happens on a deletion request prior to any resources being deleted from Kubernetes.
post-delete	Execution happens after all resources have been deleted from Kubernetes.
pre-upgrade	Execution happens after resources are rendered but prior to resources being updated in Kubernetes.
post-upgrade	Execution happens after resources have been upgraded in Kubernetes.
pre-rollback	Execution happens after resources have been rendered but prior to any resources in Kubernetes being rolled back.
post-rollback	Execution happens after resources have been rolled back in Kubernetes.
test	Execution occurs when the `helm test` command is run. Tests are covered in the next section.

A single resource can implement more than one hook by listing them as a comma-separated list. For example:

```
annotations:
  "helm.sh/hook": pre-install,pre-upgrade
```

Hooks can be weighted and specify a deletion policy for the resources after they have run. The weight enables more than one hook for the same event to be specified while providing an order in which they will run. This gives you the ability to ensure a deterministic order. Because Kubernetes resources are used for the execution of hooks, the resources are stored in Kubernetes even after execution has completed. The deletion policy provides you with some additional control on when to delete these resources from Kubernetes.

The following code provides example annotations specifying all three values:

```
    annotations:
      "helm.sh/hook": pre-install,pre-upgrade
      "helm.sh/hook-weight": "1"
      "helm.sh/hook-delete-policy": before-hook-creation,hook-succeeded
```

The weight, specified by the `helm.sh/hook-weight` annotation key, is a number represented as a string. It should always be a string. The weight can be a positive or negative number and has a default value of 0. Prior to executing hooks, Helm sorts them in ascending order.

The deletion policy, set using the annotation key `helm.sh/hook-delete-policy`, is a comma-separated list of policy options. The three possible deletion policies are found in Table 6-2.

Table 6-2. Helm hook deletion policies

Policy value	Description
before-hook-creation	The previous resource is deleted before a new instance of this hook is launched. This is the default.
hook-succeeded	Delete the Kubernetes resource after the hook is successfully run.
hook-failed	Delete the Kubernetes resource if the hook failed while executing.

By default, Helm keeps the Kubernetes resources used for hooks until the hook is run again. This provides the ability to inspect the logs or look at other information about a hook after it is run. A common policy to set is the one used in the previous example. This will keep hook resources around unless they complete successfully. When hooks fail, the resources and their logs are still available for inspection, but otherwise they are deleted.

The following `Pod` is an example of a hook running post-install:

```
apiVersion: v1
kind: Pod
metadata:
  name: "{{ include "mychart.fullname" . }}-post-install"
  labels:
    {{- include "mychart.labels" . | nindent 4 }}
  annotations:
    "helm.sh/hook": post-install
    "helm.sh/hook-weight": "-1"
    "helm.sh/hook-delete-policy": before-hook-creation,hook-succeeded
spec:
  containers:
    - name: wget
      image: busybox
      command: ["/bin/sleep","{{ default "10" .Values.sleepTime }}"]
  restartPolicy: Never
```

If you are running a Helm command, such as `helm install`, and want to skip running hooks, the `--no-hooks` flag can be used. This flag is available on commands that have hooks and will cause Helm to skip executing them. Hooks are an opt-out feature.

Adding Tests to Charts

Testing is an integral part of software development, and Helm provides the ability to test charts through the use of the *test* hook and Kubernetes resources. That means tests run in a Kubernetes cluster right alongside the workloads with access to the components installed by the chart. In addition to the chart testing built into Helm, the Helm project provides an additional testing tool named Chart Testing. Since Chart Testing builds upon the features in the Helm client, we will first look at the functionality built into the Helm client.

Helm Test

Helm has a `helm test` command that executes test hooks on a running instance of a chart. The resources implementing those hooks can check database access, that database schemas are properly in place, for working connections between workloads, and other operational details.

If a test fails, Helm will exit with a nonzero exit code and provide you with the name of the Kubernetes resource that failed. The nonzero exit code is useful when paired with some automation testing systems that detect failures this way. When you have the name of the Kubernetes resource, you can look at the logs to see what failed.

Tests typically live in the *tests* subdirectory of the *templates* directory. Putting the tests in this directory provides a useful separation. This is a convention and not required for tests to run.

To illustrate a test, we will look at the *booster* chart (*https://oreil.ly/COJ7w*). In the *templates/tests* directory, there is a single test in the file *test-connection.yaml* that contains the following test hook:

```
apiVersion: v1
kind: Pod
metadata:
  name: "{{ include "booster.fullname" . }}-test-connection"
  labels:
    {{- include "booster.labels" . | nindent 4 }}
  annotations:
    "helm.sh/hook": test
spec:
  containers:
    - name: wget
      image: busybox
      command: ['wget']
      args: ['{{ include "booster.fullname" . }}:{{ .Values.service.port }}']
  restartPolicy: Never
```

This test is the one created by default for Nginx when `helm create` is run. It happens to work to test connectivity to the booster application, as well. This simple test illustrates the structure of a test.

 If you look at tests in some existing charts you might find the hook they use is `test-success` instead of `test`. In Helm version 2 there was a hook named `test-success` for running tests. Helm version 3 provides backward compatibility and will run this hook name as a test.

There are two steps to run tests. The first step is to install the chart so that an instance of it is running. You can use the `helm install` command to do this. The following command installs the *booster* chart and assumes you are running it from the root directory of the chart:

```
$ helm install boost .
```

Once the instance of the chart is running, you run the `helm test` command to execute the tests:

```
$ helm test boost
```

Helm will output the status of the test as it executes and then information about the test and the release when complete. For the previous test it would return:

```
Pod boost-booster-test-connection pending
Pod boost-booster-test-connection pending
Pod boost-booster-test-connection running
Pod boost-booster-test-connection succeeded
NAME: boost
LAST DEPLOYED: Tue Jul 21 06:47:05 2020
NAMESPACE: default
STATUS: deployed
REVISION: 1
TEST SUITE:     boost-booster-test-connection
Last Started:   Tue Jul 21 06:47:12 2020
Last Completed: Tue Jul 21 06:47:17 2020
Phase:          Succeeded
NOTES:
1. Get the application URL by running these commands:
   export POD_NAME=$(kubectl get pods --namespace default -l
     "app.kubernetes.io/name=booster,app.kubernetes.io/instance=boost"
     -o jsonpath="{.items[0].metadata.name}")
   echo "Visit http://127.0.0.1:8080 to use your application"
   kubectl --namespace default port-forward $POD_NAME 8080:80
```

When charts have dependencies that have tests, those will be run, as well. For example, if the tests in the *rocket* chart used earlier in the chapter are run, the *booster* chart tests and the *rocket* chart tests will be run.

If you need to have configuration installed as part of a test, you can put the test hook on a Kubernetes `Secret` or ConfigMap to have it installed with other test resources.

Testing charts is a great way to ensure the contents of a chart are able to get the workload running in Kubernetes and catch changes that may break that.

Chart Testing Tool

The Helm project provides an additional testing tool, built on the foundation of `helm test`, that provides more advanced testing capabilities. Some of the additional features it includes are:

- The ability to test different—mutually exclusive—configuration options at install time for a chart.

- *Chart.yaml* schema validation that includes custom schema rules.

- Additional YAML linting that includes configurable rules. For example, you can make sure indentation in the YAML files is consistent.

- When the source is stored in Git, the ability to check if the `version` property in a *Chart.yaml* file has been properly incremented.

- The ability to work with collections of charts and only test those that have changed.

The Chart Testing tool was designed to use in continuous integration system workflows, and some of the features directly target this situation.

History of Chart Testing

When Helm was in its early days, the project maintainers started a repository with some charts to showcase what you could do with charts. Helm repositories were designed to be distributed from the start—with different organizations running their own repositories—and the Helm project provided an example of how to do this.

This chart repository grew to have many charts and became a form of central repository. To aid in maintaining the many charts, automation scripts were created to help automatically provide feedback to proposed pull requests to the charts.

The automation scripts proved to be useful to more than the Helm project. To enable the chart repositories hosted by others to have the same testing capabilities, the scripts used by the Helm project were broken out into a separate tool and rewritten with portability in mind.

> The Chart Testing tool is now used by a variety of companies and organizations to aid in the testing of their hosted charts.

The ability for Chart Testing to test a chart with different, mutually exclusive, configurations requires knowing those configurations. These are bundled in the *ci* directory of a chart.

In the *ci* directory you can create a values file for each situation to test. You need to use the glob naming pattern **-values.yaml* when you name each file. For example, you can use file names like *minimal-values.yaml* and *full-values.yaml*.

Chart Testing will test each of these configurations separately. For example, when the chart is being linted, each case will be linted separately. The custom values will be passed to `helm lint` using the `--values` flag. The same idea and flag applies when the chart is being runtime tested. The values are passed to Helm using the `--values` flag beacuse this is how end users, who install the chart, provide their custom configuration.

If you want to test using various configurations but do not want to ship those configurations as part of the chart archive, you can put the *ci* directory in the *.helmignore* file. When Helm packages the chart, the *ci* directory will be ignored.

Chart Testing can be installed and used in various ways. For example, you can use it as a binary application on a development system or in a container within a continuous integration system. Learn more about using and setting it up for your situation on the project page (*https://oreil.ly/sJXpR*).

Security Considerations

Some of the biggest and most trusted technology organizations have had their users be attacked through software updates. Software changes and the mechanisms used to update and even install software provide a channel of attack.

Helm provides an opt-in means to check the provenance and integrity of charts. *Provenance* provides a means to verify the origin, such as a company or person, of a chart while *integrity* provides a way to check that you received what you expected without alterations. This functionality enables you and those who use your charts to verify who they came from and that the contents have not changed.

To accomplish this Helm uses Pretty Good Privacy (PGP), hashes, and a provenance file that sits alongside the chart archive file. For example, if you have a chart archive named *mylib-1.0.0.tgz*, you can have a provenance file named *mylib-1.0.0.tgz.prov*. This file contains a PGP message with the contents of the *Chart.yaml* file along with the hash of the chart archive. Helm can generate these files for you. The following example is the provenance file for *mylib-1.0.0.tgz*:

```
-----BEGIN PGP SIGNED MESSAGE-----
Hash: SHA512

apiVersion: v2
description: an example library chart
name: mylib
type: library
version: 0.1.0

...
files:
  mylib-0.1.0.tgz: sha256:d312aea39acf7026f39edebd315a11a52d29a9
                        6a8d68737ead110ac0c0a1163d
-----BEGIN PGP SIGNATURE-----
```

```
iQIzBAEBCgAdFiEEcR8o1RDh4Ly9X2v+lDboC/ukaQkFAl8yiesACgkQlDboC/uk
aQkG2BAAlIEgGI7uu9Kr8j4ZIxDseLmgphhPM1kgnIMPriLieBxFXSJQxciN3+dx
OQpIfdsFQvW98EnJ4781Pm+leHY2iI/L08O1cQWUtzKhfPEWC65YQJPXkTKpHnC2
wXYVUVYWvhx6BJ77RiS/f+hoXiC+i1aBqqS0TAG+AqXuwARO2tY/L7cF6EHjsUwD
pPuTNpYZ/OEWqh1KEYZYVDvLm6uN6QjV4pNTFfAgnvMckfoDLQ+kOPQVqCeUWG3F
tZO3sBzUg+Ak2dDviSTOFQ7TCifc3tOOaWS1XtcooSOkUENmTeeWV56jZnhK1rT4
yaIGT16zXZIdmkZ1t5o9VccuAhQ1Us2FhipdGqpD8yDoJABVz/ee9d2zoX8anfR7
LZ7fwecgQ/THnj54RroyQlzf2aottFiL9ZV4MjUqs0CSoA9+SZ/CcJDd/rxBGI8C
yxRqo0VoNdjT8Kr9hha13krfwD8IpLH8bv4kWt3Ckh6rgphjUL19xyTHJY7w2toY
bAeZMl3Y05Ca76EA7XDdoltE57SUS1Zzd+wDRzRD0IZO8KVk+Z5/PzzvV4l9lnDJ
X63fptInbJpyk0xYKLMFquOY7Yy5mlI9de7424CScePo9Nua3GAakfi4zk3i4Auz
2eaoU/S5uXt605OydkSLLz99BAyJwmazzf/qPyYcPWMw/b+gHxw=
=pRcC
```
```
-----END PGP SIGNATURE-----
```

A provenance file is a PGP signed message with a particular structure in the message. That hash in the message is used by Helm to validate integrity, and the PGP signature is used to validate who it came from.

There are two steps to using provenance files. First, you need to generate them. In order to do that you need to have a PGP key pair.

When creating a package using the `helm package` command, you can tell Helm to sign the package:

```
$ helm package --sign --key 'bugs@acme.example.com' \
  --keyring path/to/keyring mychart
```

The additional flags will tell Helm to create the provenance file. The `--sign` flag opts-in to signing, the `--key` flag specifies the name of the private key to use, and the `--keyring` flag specifies the location of the keyring to use that contains the private key to use for signing. When Helm creates the archive of the chart, it will also create the *.prov* file alongside it.

The provenance file should then be uploaded alongside the chart archive and made available for download from a chart repository.

Verifying happens in reverse and is built into commands such as `helm install`, `helm upgrade`, and `helm pull` along with being available in the `helm verify` command.

Helm can handle the situation where you have both the archive and provenance file locally available and when you have the chart in a remote repository.

To illustrate the situation of having both files locally, we can use the `helm verify` command:

```
$ helm verify --keyring path/to/keyring mychart-0.1.0.tgz
```

The `verify` command will tell Helm to check the hash and signature. The `--keyring` flag tells Helm where a PGP keyring exists with the public key that matches the private key the chart was signed with. This can be either a keyring or a non-ASCII-Armored version of the public key. Helm will look for the *mychart-0.1.0.tgz.prov* file and use that to perform the check.

Running the `verify` command on the *mylib* chart would look like:

```
$ helm verify mylib-0.1.0.tgz --keyring public.key
```

This would output:

```
Signed by: Matthew Farina
Using Key With Fingerprint: 672C657BE06B4B30969C4A57461449C25E36B98E
Chart Hash Verified: sha256:d312aea39acf7026f39edebd315a11a52d29a96a8d68737ead11
                     0ac0c0a1163d
```

If you have a chart in a Helm repository, Helm will download the provenance file when it downloads the chart. For example:

```
$ helm install --verify --keyring public.key myrepo/mychart
```

When Helm fetches the chart archive, it will also download the provenance file, verify the signature, and verify the hash.

 The public key should be shared through a different channel from the chart and provenance file.

If there is a problem during the verification process, Helm will provide an error and exit with a nonzero exit code.

GNU Privacy Guard

Starting in GNU Privacy Guard (GPG) 2.1, keys were stored in a new keybox format. This new format is incompatible with PGP specifications and formats. That means

there are some extra steps to working with keys if you use GPG. The following commands provide a reference you can use when working with GPG.

You can export your secret keys from GPG into a PGP format with:

```
gpg --export-secret-keys > secring.gpg
```

You can export public keys from GPG into a PGP format with:

```
gpg --export > pubring.gpg
```

You can convert a public key in ASCII-Armor format to binary format with:

```
gpg --dearmor < pgp_key.asc > public.key
```

pgp_key.asc is the name of the ASCII-Armored key file and *public.key* is the name of
the same key in binary format. This *public.key* file can be passed to Helm as a keyring
for verification.

If you use a password or a hardware security device with GPG, you may not be able to
export your private key. In that case, there is the Helm GPG plugin (*https://oreil.ly/
pEJh3*). It provides commands and a means to directly work with provenance files
through GPG. Plugins are covered in more detail in Chapter 8.

Verifying that a chart came from who you expected and that the content hasn't
changed is a useful step in securing your software supply chain.

Custom Resource Definitions

Kubernetes custom resource definitions (CRDs) provide a means to extend the
Kubernetes API, and Helm provides methods to install them as part of the chart.

Custom Resource Definitions, the Kubernetes API, and Some Gotchas

CRDs provide a method to extend the Kubernetes API for all users of a cluster. They
add new resource types, known as custom resources, that can be uploaded to a cluster
alongside the resource types that ship with Kubernetes. CRDs provide a schema and
can describe multiple versions of the same resource. They are a shared global
resource.

CRDs in a cluster can be updated to change an API. This can be to change or update
the schema for an existing version of an API or to add new versions to the API. The
Kubernetes community recommends that the API version be incremented anytime
there is a breaking change to an API, but backward compatible changes are accepta-
ble. There is no enforcement of this recommendation within Kubernetes. For example, adding an optional field to an API is backward compatible, but a new mandatory
field is not. Changes to CRDs affect all users of the cluster.

When a CRD is deleted from a cluster, all of the custom resources based on it are deleted as well. This applies to all users of the cluster because CRDs are cluster-wide resources. In multitenant clusters, when one tenant deletes a CRD the custom resources described by that CRD for all tenants are deleted.

CRDs work this way because they were designed to be cluster-level extensions. In a retrospective on CRDs, Brendan Burns, one of Kubernetes' founders, described their three goals as:

1. An easy method to dynamically add new API types to Kubernetes.

2. To enable API extensibility without significant additional load on operators of Kubernetes clusters.

3. Enable an ecosystem of value add extensions to end-user clusters.

When Kubernetes API extensions were being developed, another method to extend the API was developed that required a lot more work from cluster operators and those developing extensions. CRDs simplified the experience.

CRDs are conceptually similar to kernel modules and extensions in operating systems.

There are two Helm-based methods to managing the CRDs used by a chart. Choosing between the methods to use often depends on the requirements and environment configurations of those who need to install your charts.

First, the *crds* directory is a special directory you can add to a chart to hold your CRDs. Helm will install CRDs prior to installing other resources. This ensures that CRDs are available for any custom resources or controllers that may leverage them in the chart.

CRDs in the *crds* directory are different from other resources installed by Helm. These files are not templated. This is useful for the CRD management workflows we will cover in a moment. Helm will not upgrade or delete CRDs like it does other resources. Upgrading CRDs changes the API surface for all instances of the custom resources in the cluster, and deleting CRDs removes all of the custom resources for all users. When it comes to handling these cluster-wide changes you will need to use a companion tool, like kubectl, the command-line tool for Kubernetes.

Because CRDs change the Kubernetes API, whoever is installing your chart may not have permission to install, upgrade, or delete them. This is the case if you are bundling an application for distribution to other companies or the general public. Some cluster administrators restrict access to these functions as part of their access controls for security.

The CRDs in the *crds* directory can be extracted from a chart and used directly with tools like `kubectl`. This enables the CRDs to be passed to someone with permission to install them, if the person installing the chart doesn't have permission. The extracted CRDs can also be used to upgrade the CRDs within a cluster using other tools.

A second, Helm-based, way to manage CRDs while providing an ordering that installs CRDs before using them through custom resources is to use a second chart that holds the CRDs. This method provides more nuanced control through Helm.

Using a second chart will let you:

1. Use Helm templates and the normal *templates* directory for CRDs.
2. Helm will manage the life cycle of the CRDs. That includes uninstalling and upgrades. If you want to keep the CRD installed after the chart is uninstalled, you can set the annotation `"helm.sh/resource-policy"`: `keep` to tell Helm to skip uninstalling the resource.
3. If you have issues with an application and use the uninstall and reinstall method to try to fix issues, the CRDs in the separate chart will not be deleted.

This second chart can be installed with either a loose coupling, where the directions tell people to install it first, or a tight coupling, where it is set as a dependency. If the chart holding the CRDs is set as a dependency the use case should be that it is only installed once as it is setting cluster-wide resources.

When Helm is managing the CRDs, special care needs to be given for handling upgrade and delete cases. For example, if two versions of the CRD installing chart are installed, as you need to ensure an older version doesn't overwrite a newer version and that a newer version doesn't break the functionality for someone else in the cluster using the older version. This can happen if two people install different versions of the chart that installs CRDs. In multitenant clusters different users of the cluster may not know about each other, and it's important to ensure that one user of the cluster does not break the workloads of another user of the cluster.

When installing and working with CRDs, the Helm developers recommend taking special care in all of the life cycle steps to make sure that users of charts don't run into situations that accidentally break production workloads.

Conclusion

Helm charts are more than a collection of templates. They handle dependencies, can include schemas, provide an event hook mechanism, can include tests, and have features for security. These features are part of what make Helm a robust and reliable solution to the package management problem.

## CHAPTER 7

Chart Repositories

No package manager is complete without a way to share and distribute the packages themselves. Organizations and vendors must have a way to publish packages for end users to download and consume. Likewise, end users must have a common way to fetch packages from a variety of sources.

Helm enables package distribution though a system called chart repositories. Chart repositories are simple HTTP(S) web services from which users can discover and download available charts. Conceptually, chart repositories are similar in design to Debian package repositories, Fedora package databases, or the Comprehensive Perl Archive Network (CPAN).

In this chapter, we will first dive deep into the internals of a chart repository. We will discuss the repository index and how to update it with new chart versions. After that, we will show how to set up a chart repository from scratch, how to secure one, and also show a real-world example of how to host a public chart repository using GitHub Pages for open source projects. After this, we will walk through the various helm repo commands and how to use them effectively.

Toward the end of the chapter, we will cover the next generation of chart repositories using Helm's experimental Open Container Initiative (OCI) support. This bleeding-edge functionality added in Helm 3 allows users to store Helm charts in container registries alongside their container images.

Lastly, we will briefly describe some of the projects in the Helm ecosystem related to chart repositories.

The Repository Index

All chart repositories contain a special repository index file called *index.yaml*, which lists all available charts and their respective download locations.

 See Appendix B for more details describing the format of *index.yaml*.

Here's an example of a very basic *index.yaml* file:

```
apiVersion: v1
entries:
  superapp:
  - apiVersion: v2
    appVersion: 1.16.0
    created: "2020-04-27T17:46:52.60919-05:00"
    description: A Helm chart for Kubernetes
    digest: cd1f8d949aeb6a7a3c6720bfe71688d4add794881b78ad9715017581f7867db4
    name: superapp
    type: application
    urls:
    - superapp-0.1.0.tgz
    version: 0.1.0
generated: "2020-04-27T17:46:52.607943-05:00"
```

Note the `entries` section, which lists all charts and chart versions. This *index.yaml* example lists a just single chart, *superapp*, with a single version, 0.1.0.

An Example of a Chart Repository Index

Usually, chart repositories list many charts and all their available versions. This allows users to download a specific version of the chart they wish to install. The following is a more real-world example of a chart repository index, containing multiple charts and chart versions:

```
apiVersion: v1
entries:
  cert-manager:
  - apiVersion: v1
    appVersion: v0.14.2
    created: "2020-04-08T11:38:26.281Z"
    description: A Helm chart for cert-manager
    digest: 160e1bd4906855b91c8ba42afe10af2d0443b184916e4534175890b1a7278f4e
    home: https://github.com/jetstack/cert-manager
    icon: https://raw.githubusercontent.com/jetstack/cert-manager/master/logo/
        logo.png
    keywords:
```

```
  - cert-manager
  - kube-lego
  - letsencrypt
  - tls
  maintainers:
  - email: dev@jetstack.io
    name: jetstack-dev
  name: cert-manager
  sources:
  - https://github.com/jetstack/cert-manager
  urls:
  - charts/cert-manager-v0.14.2.tgz
  version: v0.14.2
- apiVersion: v1
  appVersion: v0.14.1
  created: "2020-03-25T18:30:16.354Z"
  description: A Helm chart for cert-manager
  digest: 629150400487df41af6c7acf2a3bfd8e691f657a930bc81e1dcf3b9d23329baf
  home: https://github.com/jetstack/cert-manager
  icon: https://raw.githubusercontent.com/jetstack/cert-manager/master/logo/
        logo.png
  keywords:
  - cert-manager
  - kube-lego
  - letsencrypt
  - tls
  maintainers:
  - email: dev@jetstack.io
    name: jetstack-dev
  name: cert-manager
  sources:
  - https://github.com/jetstack/cert-manager
  urls:
  - charts/cert-manager-v0.14.1.tgz
  version: v0.14.1
tor-proxy:
- apiVersion: v1
  created: "2018-11-16T09:23:13.538Z"
  description: A Helm chart for Kubernetes
  digest: 1d2fd11e22ba58bf0a263c39777f0f18855368b099aed7b03123ca91e55343e4
  name: tor-proxy
  urls:
  - charts/tor-proxy-0.1.1.tgz
  version: 0.1.1
generated: "2020-04-23T17:43:41Z"
```

The preceding example shows two available charts: *cert-manager* and *tor-proxy*. There are a total of three available chart versions: *cert-manager* v0.14.1, *cert-manager* v0.14.2 (latest), and *tor-proxy* 0.1.1 (latest). The latest versions of each chart in the repo are displayed when running a `helm search`.

Typically chart archives (*.tgz* files) themselves are served from the same location as the repository index, but the index may also link to remote locations on entirely different domains. Here is a snippet from an *index.yaml* referencing chart archives located on a separate domain (note the absolute URL):

```
...
- appVersion: 2.10.1
  created: 2019-01-14T23:25:37.125126859Z
  description: A simple, powerful publishing platform that allows you to share
    your stories with the world
  digest: dcadf39f81253a9a016fcab1b74aba1d470e015197152affdaeb1b337221cc5c
  engine: gotpl
  home: http://www.ghost.org/
  icon: https://bitnami.com/assets/stacks/ghost/img/ghost-stack-220x234.png
  keywords:
  - ghost
  - blog
  - http
  - web
  - application
  - nodejs
  - javascript
  maintainers:
  - email: containers@bitnami.com
    name: Bitnami
  name: ghost
  sources:
  - https://github.com/bitnami/bitnami-docker-ghost
  urls:
  - https://charts.example.com/ghost-6.2.3.tgz  ❶
  version: 6.2.3
...
```

❶ Absolute chart URL

Other fields found in each entry include the metadata for a chart as described in *Chart.yaml*, such as `description`, as well as an added digest field containing the Secure Hash Algorithm (SHA-256) checksum of the chart archive. In Chapter 4 we covered chart metadata and *Chart.yaml* in detail.

Additionally, at the top level is a `generated` field describing when the index was created (in RFC 3339 format), as well as an `apiVersion` describing the API version of the index. At the time of writing, there is currently only one API version for chart repositories. This field should always be `v1`.

Generating an Index

The repository index can be generated by a custom program, or typed out manually. Helm also provides built-in functionality to generate the repository index for you.

Let's create an empty directory, *charts/*, which will serve as the root of our chart repository:

```
$ mkdir -p charts/
```

To generate a repository index inside the *charts/* directory, run the following:

```
$ helm repo index charts/
```

This will create a file at *charts/index.yaml*. Let's take a look:

```
$ cat charts/index.yaml
apiVersion: v1
entries: {}
generated: "2020-04-28T09:55:29.517285-05:00"
```

You'll notice that the `entries` are empty. This is expected because we do not yet have any charts in the *charts/* directory.

Let's create a sample chart, and package it into the *charts/* directory:

```
$ helm create superapp
Creating superapp
$ helm package superapp/ --destination charts/
Successfully packaged chart and saved it to: charts/superapp-0.1.0.tgz
```

Now let's try generating the index again:

```
$ helm repo index charts/
$ cat charts/index.yaml
apiVersion: v1
  entries:
    superapp:
    - apiVersion: v2
      appVersion: 1.16.0
      created: "2020-04-28T10:12:22.507943-05:00"
      description: A Helm chart for Kubernetes
      digest: 46f9ddeca12ec0bc257a702dac7d069af018aed2a87314d86b230454ac033672
      name: superapp
      type: application
      urls:
      - superapp-0.1.0.tgz
      version: 0.1.0
generated: "2020-04-28T10:12:22.507289-05:00"
```

Now we see our chart listed in the `entries` section.

Adding to an Existing Index

In some scenarios (continuous integration/continuous deployment [CI/CD], for example), you may only have access to an existing *index.yaml* file and a newly packaged chart archive. Helm provides a mechanism for building upon the contents of an existing index with the `--merge` option.

Let's simulate this scenario. Create a new directory called *workspace/*, which will represent a new working directory in a CI/CD pipeline:

```
$ mkdir -p workspace/
```

Copy the existing index file into the *workspace/* directory with a new name, such as *index-old.yaml*:

```
$ cp charts/index.yaml workspace/index-old.yaml
```

In a real-world scenario, you might source the existing index file from some remote location (e.g., Amazon S3).

Next let's create another Helm chart and package it into the *workspace/* directory:

```
$ helm create duperapp
Creating duperapp
$ helm package duperapp/ --destination workspace/
Successfully packaged chart and saved it to: workspace/duperapp-0.1.0.tgz
```

Run the following command, which will create a new *index.yaml* file based on the combination of the existing entries found in *index-old.yaml*, as well as any *.tgz* files in the *workspace/* directory:

```
$ helm repo index workspace/ --merge workspace/index-old.yaml
```

Finally, move the files from the *workspace/* directory into the *charts/* directory, overwriting the old index file with the new one:

```
$ mv workspace/duperapp-0.1.0.tgz charts/
$ mv workspace/index.yaml charts/
```

The new version of the index file should now contain entries for both charts:

```
$ cat charts/index.yaml
apiVersion: v1
entries:
  duperapp:
  - apiVersion: v2
    appVersion: 1.16.0
    created: "2020-04-28T11:34:26.780267-05:00"
    description: A Helm chart for Kubernetes
    digest: 30ea14a4ce92e0d1aea7626cb30dfbac68a87dca360d0d76a55460b004d62f52
    name: duperapp
    type: application
    urls:
    - duperapp-0.1.0.tgz
    version: 0.1.0
  superapp:
  - apiVersion: v2
    appVersion: 1.16.0
    created: "2020-04-28T10:12:22.507943-05:00"
    description: A Helm chart for Kubernetes
    digest: 46f9ddeca12ec0bc257a702dac7d069af018aed2a87314d86b230454ac033672
```

```
      name: superapp
      type: application
      urls:
      - superapp-0.1.0.tgz
      version: 0.1.0
  generated: "2020-04-28T11:34:26.779758-05:00"
```

This method is useful in environments where you do not necessarily have access to a directory containing all of the chart archives.

Keep in mind, however, that if this merge occurs on multiple systems at the same time, you may run into a race condition where one or more charts goes missing from the index. This can be mitigated by ensuring that this process is only performed synchronously (e.g., a single CI job responsible for creating *index.yaml* for the repository). Another way to address this problem is to use a dynamic web server that is responsible for generating the contents of *index.yaml*. The *ChartMuseum* project, which is described later in this chapter in "Related Projects" on page 148, is one such example of a dynamic chart repository server you can use for this purpose.

Setting Up a Chart Repository

One of the benefits of chart repositories is that they can be entirely static—meaning you can place the files behind a simple web server such as Apache or Nginx and serve them as is. You can even use object storage providers, such as Amazon S3. No significant computation needs to occur on the server side when a client requests *index.yaml*, for example. The static web server just opens the file as it exists on the filesystem and sends the raw contents back to the client.

A Simple Chart Repository with Python

For the sake of this example, we will use Python's built-in static web server to start up a local test repository. Note that almost all programming languages have some support in their standard libraries to start a web server and serve static files. Python is chosen simply because it comes preinstalled on most Unix-based systems, and because it provides an easy one-line command to start a static web server.

Follow the instructions in the previous section ("Generating an Index" on page 130) to create the *charts/* directory, containing the files *index.yaml*, *superapp-0.1.0.tgz*, and *duperapp-0.1.0.tgz*. Run one of the following commands to start a local web server at *http://localhost:8080*.

Using Python 3 (try this first):

```
$ ( cd charts/ && python3 -m http.server --bind 127.0.0.1 8080 )
```

Using Python 2:

```
$ ( ch charts/ && python -m SimpleHTTPServer 8080 )
```

The Python 2 version of this command listens on all interfaces (0.0.0.0) versus just the loopback interface (127.0.0.1). Depending on your system, this will allow other devices on your network to connect. Be mindful of which files are present in the *charts/* directory before running this command.

Now, in another terminal window, try fetching *index.yaml* using `curl`:

```
$ curl -sO http://localhost:8080/index.yaml
$ ls *.yaml
index.yaml
```

Now let's verify that we can fetch chart archives:

```
$ curl -sO http://localhost:8080/superapp-0.1.0.tgz
$ curl -sO http://localhost:8080/duperapp-0.1.0.tgz
$ ls *.tgz
duperapp-0.1.0.tgz       superapp-0.1.0.tgz
```

If the `curl` commands succeed, your chart repository is ready to be used with Helm.

Securing a Chart Repository

In many cases, you may wish to limit access to a chart repository or maintain an audit trail of which users are accessing which resources. Helm has built-in support to allow users to authenticate themselves against chart repositories protected by either basic auth or mTLS.

Basic auth

Chart repositories can be protected by basic access authentication, or *basic auth*. This requires that users provide a valid username/password combination to access resources on the server.

Basic auth can be implemented by a server by first checking the `Authorization` header prior to processing a request. An incoming basic auth header resembles the following:

```
Authorization: Basic bXl1c2VyOm15cGFzcw==  ❶
```

❶ The opaque string here is the Base64 encoding of *username* + ":" + *password*.

 The contents of the `Authorization` header are *not* encrypted, so you are strongly encouraged to also use HTTPS when supplying basic auth credentials.

When adding a repository for the first time, you can supply a username and password combination on the command line, which will instruct Helm to use basic auth when making requests against this repository:

```
$ helm repo add mycharts http://localhost:8080 --username myuser \
    --password mypass
"mycharts" has been added to your repositories
```

Client certificates

Most client-server communication over HTTPS allows the client to verify the identity of the server based on the SSL certificate provided by the server. With mutual TLS authentication (mTLS), servers can also verify the identity of the client based on a separate SSL certificate presented by the client during the TLS handshake.

Here is a simple Nginx server configuration enabling mTLS for a chart repository, assuming static files (i.e., *index.yaml*, *.tgz* files) are located in the directory */chartrepo* on the server:

```
events { }
http {
    server {
        root /chartrepo;
        listen 443 ssl;
        server_name charts.example.com;
        ssl_certificate /certs/server.crt;        ❶
        ssl_certificate_key /certs/server.key;     ❷
        ssl_client_certificate /certs/client-ca.pem;  ❸
        ssl_verify_client on;
        proxy_set_header SSL_CLIENT_CERT $ssl_client_cert;
    }
}
```

❶ Server's SSL certificate

❷ Server's private key

❸ Certificate authority (CA) for client authentication—only requests from clients with a certificate signed by this CA will be accepted

The first step in obtaining a client certificate is to generate a new private key and certificate signing request (CSR):

```
$ mkdir -p ~/client-certs/
$ cd ~/client-certs/
$ openssl genrsa -out francis.key 4096
$ openssl req -new -key francis.key -out francis.csr
```

When prompted for a "Common Name" when generating the CSR, you must enter a value. Use something that identifies the client (e.g., "francis"). Other fields can technically be left blank, although you are encouraged to fill them out.

Next, using the certificate authority configured on the server (`client-ca.pem`) and the associated private key (`client-ca.key`), generate a new client certificate from the CSR:

```
$ openssl x509 -req -in francis.csr \
    -CA /certs/client-ca.pem -CAkey /certs/client-ca.key \
    -out francis.crt -sha256
```

Now you can use this certificate to authenticate by specifying the `--cert-file` and `--key-file` options upon adding a new chart repository:

```
$ helm repo add client-cert-repo https://charts.example.com \
    --cert-file ~/client-certs/francis.crt --key-file ~/client-certs/francis.key
"client-cert-repo" has been added to your repositories
```

In the case that your server is using a self-signed certificate, you can also specify the `--ca-file` option pointing to a trusted certificate or certificate bundle:

```
$ helm repo add client-cert-repo-selfsigned https://charts.example.com \
    --cert-file ~/client-certs/francis.crt --key-file ~/client-certs/francis.key
    --ca-file /certs/server.crt
"client-cert-repo-selfsigned" has been added to your repositories
```

 The paths used for `--cert-file`, `--key-file`, and `--ca-file` are all stored in the Helm cache tied to the repository. It is important not to move these files; otherwise, future requests to the repository will fail due to missing files needed for the client to authenticate.

For more information on mTLS, please see Internet Engineering Task Force (IETF) RFC 8446, "The Transport Layer Security (TLS) Protocol Version 1.3."

Real-World Example: Using GitHub Pages

GitHub has a free, static hosting solution called GitHub Pages. If you don't mind making your charts public to the world, GitHub Pages is a great option for hosting a chart repository as you incur zero cost.

What's even better is that GitHub Pages allows you to use a custom domain name that points to your GitHub Pages site. In this section we will show how to easily set up a public Helm chart repository using GitHub Pages.

There are some limitations on GitHub Pages (such as bandwidth), so before using this method, enumerate the performance requirements for your chart repository compared to GitHub's documentation of GitHub Pages' features.

Create a new Git repo

The first step is to create a brand-new Git repo on GitHub dedicated to your chart repository. You could technically host the chart repo alongside other content, but for the sake of simplicity, we will use a dedicated Git repo. Figure 7-1 shows how to set up a new repository.

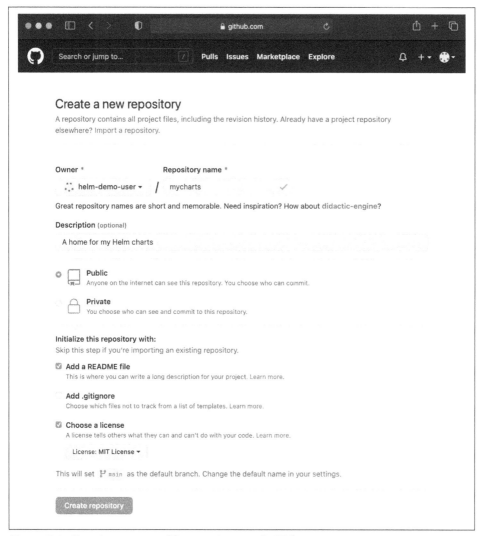

Figure 7-1. Creating a new public repository in GitHub

Once you're logged in to GitHub, click the top right of the screen and select "New repository." Name the Git repo whatever you want. We will use the name *mycharts* for this example. Make sure to select the option for marking the repository as "Public," which is a prerequisite for using GitHub Pages. Select the box for "Initialize this repository with a README," which will allow us to clone the repo immediately. Feel free to select a license such as "MIT License" to indicate that the source code in this repo is free to use and repurpose. Finally, click "Create repository."

 It's important to note in this context the difference between a Helm repo (or chart repository) and a Git repo hosted on GitHub, which is used for version control.

Enable GitHub Pages

Navigate to the Settings panel on the repository. In the main settings, scroll down to the section titled GitHub Pages (see Figure 7-2). For the Source option, select "main branch." This will cause GitHub to redeploy your GitHub Pages site every time you make a new commit to the main branch. Click Save.

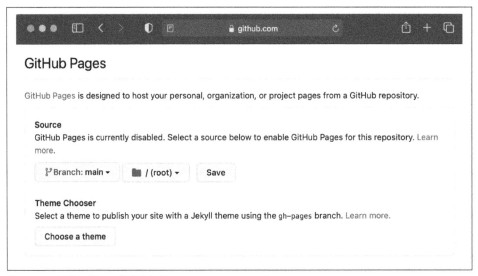

Figure 7-2. Enabling GitHub Pages on your repository

Optional: Use a custom domain

Sites on GitHub Pages, by default, are hosted as a subdomain on the github.io domain. For example, the URL to your site would resemble something like *https://yourusername.github.io/mycharts/*.

If you have a custom domain name to use, in your registrar's web console (or alternatively, in the console for the service you have set up to use for your authoritative nameservers), create a new DNS record pointing to *yourusername.github.io*. If using the root domain, use an ALIAS record type; otherwise, for subdomains, use a CNAME record type.

Go back to your repository settings in GitHub. As in Figure 7-3, in the "Custom domain" input, enter your domain that you set up a DNS record for.

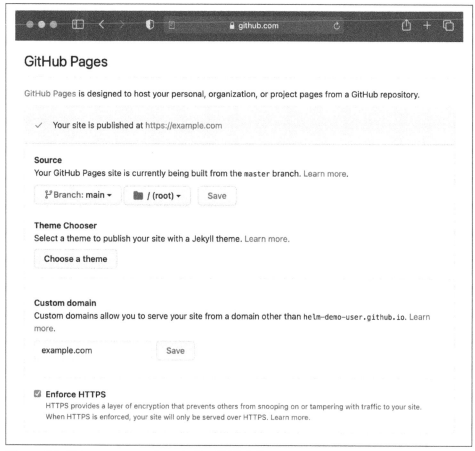

Figure 7-3. Using a custom domain for GitHub Pages

It may take up to an hour for GitHub to generate a TLS certificate for your domain. Once it is ready, you should see some text displayed in the settings such as "Your site is published at https://example.com." Once you see this, make sure to enable the Enforce HTTPS option so that your site is only ever accessed over HTTPS versus just plain HTTP.

Adding chart repository files

Locate the clone URL for your repo in the GitHub UI (typically on the right side of the screen). Clone your new GitHub repository to your local system so that we can add some files to turn it into a real chart repository:

```
$ git clone git@github.com:youruser/mycharts.git
Cloning into 'mycharts'...
remote: Enumerating objects: 7, done.
remote: Counting objects: 100% (7/7), done.
remote: Compressing objects: 100% (6/6), done.
remote: Total 7 (delta 0), reused 0 (delta 0), pack-reused 0
Receiving objects: 100% (7/7), done.
```

Enter the directory of your Git repository:

```
$ cd mycharts/
```

Next, let's create a chart called *pineapple* in a new *src/* directory, package it into an archive in the root of the repo, and create an *index.yaml* file:

```
$ mkdir -p src/
$ helm create src/pineapple
Creating src/pineapple
$ helm package src/pineapple/
Successfully packaged chart and saved it to: /home/user/mycharts/
    pineapple-0.1.0.tgz
$ helm repo index .
```

Once that's done, let's commit and push all these new files back to GitHub:

```
$ git add .

$ git commit -m "Add pineapple chart v0.1.0"
[main 9bba19d] Add pineapple chart v0.1.0
 13 files changed, 395 insertions(+)
 create mode 100644 index.yaml
 create mode 100644 pineapple-0.1.0.tgz
 create mode 100644 src/pineapple/.helmignore
 create mode 100644 src/pineapple/Chart.yaml
 create mode 100644 src/pineapple/templates/NOTES.txt
 create mode 100644 src/pineapple/templates/_helpers.tpl
 create mode 100644 src/pineapple/templates/deployment.yaml
 create mode 100644 src/pineapple/templates/hpa.yaml
 create mode 100644 src/pineapple/templates/ingress.yaml
 create mode 100644 src/pineapple/templates/service.yaml
 create mode 100644 src/pineapple/templates/serviceaccount.yaml
 create mode 100644 src/pineapple/templates/tests/test-connection.yaml
 create mode 100644 src/pineapple/values.yaml

$ git push origin main
Enumerating objects: 20, done.
Counting objects: 100% (20/20), done.
Delta compression using up to 12 threads
Compressing objects: 100% (17/17), done.
```

```
Writing objects: 100% (19/19), 9.29 KiB | 4.64 MiB/s, done.
Total 19 (delta 0), reused 0 (delta 0)
To github.com:youruser/mycharts.git
   4964b76..9bba19d  main -> main
```

Go back to GitHub in the browser. There is a small delay between the time you push a change and those changes becoming avaiable on your GitHub Pages site. Click the Environments item in the right sidebar. This will tell you the last time your site was deployed. If you see a reference to the commit you just pushed (9bba19d in the preceding example), your GitHub Pages site is ready to use.

Using your GitHub Pages site as a chart repository

Once you have pushed an *index.yaml* file up to your Git repo, and the site is live with the latest commit, you can use it exactly as you would any other chart repository.

Add your GitHub Pages chart repository to your local repositories:

```
$ helm repo add gh-pages https://yourusername.github.io/mycharts/
```

Or, if you're using a custom domain:

```
$ helm repo add gh-pages https://example.com
```

Using Chart Repositories

Once you have a working chart repository (see previous section), you can then leverage it using the Helm CLI.

Several commands are available under the top-level helm repo subcommand for working with chart repositories. This section will focus on how to use each of these commands effectively.

Adding a Repository

The very first step in using a chart repository is to assign a unique name to it (such as mycharts) and add it to a list of repositories known by Helm. When you first add a repository, Helm fetches *index.yaml* from the URL provided and stores it locally.

Use the helm repo add command to add your repository:

```
$ helm repo add mycharts http://localhost:8080
"mycharts" has been added to your repositories
```

If you are running the Python example, check out the logs for your chart repository and you should see the incoming request for GET /index.yaml:

```
127.0.0.1 - - [06/May/2020 15:31:07] "GET /index.yaml HTTP/1.1" 200 -
```

Downloading Charts

To download a chart directly from a repository, use the `helm pull` command:

```
$ helm pull mycharts/superapp
```

Helm will automatically find the latest version based on Semantic Versioning. You can also specify a version:

```
$ helm pull mycharts/superapp --version 0.1.0
```

This will result in a new chart archive (*.tgz* file) in your workspace:

```
$ ls *.tgz
superapp-0.1.0.tgz
```

This archive can be then be installed directly:

```
$ helm install superapp-dev superapp-0.1.0.tgz
```

You can also install charts directly from added repositories:

```
$ helm install superapp-dev mycharts/superapp
```

Listing Repositories

It's oftentimes helpful to know which chart repositories have already been added on your system. Knowing this may help you decide whether you want to use one of them to download charts or to remove one of them from the system completely.

Use the `helm repo list` command to list all chart repositories added to your system:

```
$ helm repo list
NAME      URL
mycharts       http://localhost:8080
```

You can also leverage the `--output` / `-o` option to get this in machine-readable format, if needed.

Get the list as YAML by adding `-o yaml`:

```
$ helm repo list -o yaml
- name: mycharts
  url: http://localhost:8080
```

Get the list as JSON by adding `-o json`:

```
$ helm repo list -o json
[{"name":"mycharts","url":"http://localhost:8080"}]
```

Updating Repositories

Once new chart versions are released, repository owners add the *.tgz* package to the repo storage and update *index.yaml* with a new entry.

In order to fetch the latest version of the repository index, use the `helm repo update` command:

```
$ helm repo update
Hang tight while we grab the latest from your chart repositories...
...Successfully got an update from the "mycharts" chart repository
Update Complete. Happy Helming!
```

If you are running the Python example, once again, you should notice an incoming request for `GET /index.yaml` in the output logs from your chart repository:

```
127.0.0.1 - - [06/May/2020 15:31:07] "GET /index.yaml HTTP/1.1" 200 -
```

Whether or not the repository index has changed contents (we haven't added any more charts to `myrepo`), the file is fetched and downloaded into the cache, overwriting the previously saved version.

Removing a Repository

In order to remove a repository, you can use `helm repo remove`:

```
$ helm repo remove mycharts
"mycharts" has been removed from your repositories
```

This will remove all references to this repository stored in the Helm cache.

Experimental OCI Support

> Helm's OCI support (*https://oreil.ly/eH4KE*) is still considered highly experimental. While development in this area is still active, the syntax described in this section may soon become outdated.

The chart repository system was designed to be easy to use. In most cases, this system has proven to be sufficient—enabling organizations around the globe to share and distribute their Helm charts.

Chart repositories do, however, present a few key challenges:

- They have no concept of namespaces; all charts for a repo are listed in a single index
- They have no fine-grained access control; you either have access to all charts in the repo or none of them
- Chart packages with different names but the exact same raw contents are stored twice

- The repository index can become extremely large, causing Helm to consume a lot of memory

Rather than trying to add features to address all of these issues with the current chart repository model, it made much more sense to build the next generation of chart repositories on top of registries that conform to the *OCI Distribution Specification*.

OCI stands for the *Open Container Initiative*. Taken from the website at *https://open containers.org*, OCI is defined as the following:

> An open governance structure for the express purpose of creating open industry standards around container formats and runtimes.

One of the standards defined by OCI is the *distribution specification*. This spec describes an HTTP API used for distributing container images. Interestingly enough, this API is general-purpose and can apply to all sorts of things that *aren't* container images—things such as Helm charts!

Starting in Helm 3.0.0, experimental support was added to push and pull charts to and from OCI-based container registries.

History of the OCI Distribution Spec

Docker introduced its own container engine in 2013, which was challenged in 2014 by CoreOS when it introduced *rkt*, an alternative engine with an open standard. Fun fact: the concept of the Kubernetes Pod comes directly from *rkt*. In an effort to bridge the divide, the Open Container Initiative was formed in 2015 to collaborate on open standards for container runtimes and images.

Meanwhile, Docker had also been working on v2 of its registry API. If you have ever used `docker pull` or `docker push`, the underlying HTTP calls are based upon this API. Docker registries began to see massive industry adoption, giving birth to companies such as Quay.io (*https://www.quay.io*). Cloud providers such as Amazon Web Services began offering their own hosted options.

In 2018, Docker donated its registry v2 specification to OCI under the name *distribution spec* (*https://oreil.ly/JWYFv*), enabling a broader community to continue to build on top of Docker's efforts. The spec continues to evolve today as a general-purpose storage solution with a strong API.

Enabling OCI Support

At the time of writing, Helm's OCI support is still considered experimental.

For now, set the following in your environment to enable OCI support:

```
$ export HELM_EXPERIMENTAL_OCI=1
```

Running a Local Registry

The Docker Distribution project (also known as the Docker registry) was the original implementation of Docker's Registry v2 API. It supports Helm charts out of the box.

If you have docker installed, you can easily run a local registry in a container on port 5000 with the following command:

```
$ docker run -d --name oci-registry -p 5000:5000 registry
```

To tail the logs for you registry, run the following (press Ctrl-C to exit):

```
$ docker logs -f oci-registry
```

To stop your registry, run the following:

```
$ docker rm -f oci-registry
```

The Docker registry has several configuration options (*https://oreil.ly/CBb0F*) related to authentication, storage, etc.

If you wish to configure basic auth with a single username-password combo, first create a *.htpasswd* file:

```
$ htpasswd -cB -b auth.htpasswd myuser mypass
```

Then start the registry, mounting the *.htpasswd* file and setting the REGISTRY_AUTH environment variable:

```
$ docker run -d --name oci-registry -p 5000:5000 \
    -v $(pwd)/auth.htpasswd:/etc/docker/registry/auth.htpasswd \
    -e REGISTRY_AUTH="{htpasswd: {realm: localhost, path: /etc/docker/registry \
    auth.htpasswd}}" registry
```

For more information about Docker Distribution, visit the project GitHub page (*https://oreil.ly/Q8Omf*).

Logging In to a Registry

In order to authenticate against a registry, use the helm registry login command (you will be prompted to manually enter a password):

```
$ helm registry login -u myuser localhost:5000
Password:
Login succeeded
```

This makes a simple GET request to the path /v2/ on the registry using the credentials to determine if they are valid. If they are, the credentials will be stored in a Helm config file. If you have any Docker credential stores enabled (such as osxkeychain on macOS), the username and password will be stored there securely.

The example of running a local registry at localhost:5000 uses no authentication. If you haven't enabled authentication on your registry, any combination of login credentials will be accepted.

Logging Out of a Registry

In order to remove credentials for a given registry from your system, use the `helm registry logout` command:

```
$ helm registry logout localhost:5000
Logout succeeded
```

Storing a Chart in the Cache

Prior to uploading a chart to a registry, you must first save it into the cache. This converts a chart from its normal state into content-addressable blobs and also gives it a unique identifier.

Use `helm chart save` to store a chart in the cache:

```
$ helm chart save mychart/ localhost:5000/myrepo/mychart
ref:     localhost:5000/myrepo/mychart:2.7.0
digest:  1b251d38cfe948dfc0a5745b7af5ca574ecb61e52aed10b19039db39af6e1617
size:    2.4 KiB
name:    mychart
version: 2.7.0
2.7.0: saved
```

Notice that the tag used on the chart reference is based upon the chart's version in *Chart.yaml* (`2.7.0`).

You can also use a custom tag, such as `stable`, by specifying it after a colon (`:`) on the chart reference:

```
$ helm chart save mychart/ localhost:5000/myrepo/mychart:stable
ref:     localhost:5000/myrepo/mychart:stable
digest:  1b251d38cfe948dfc0a5745b7af5ca574ecb61e52aed10b19039db39af6e1617
size:    2.4 KiB
name:    mychart
version: 2.7.0
stable: saved
```

Listing Charts in the Cache

Use `helm chart list` to display all charts currently stored in the cache:

```
$ helm chart list
REF                                        VERSION DIGEST   SIZE
localhost:5000/myrepo/mychart:2.7.0        2.7.0   84059d7  454 B
```

```
localhost:5000/stable/acs-engine-autoscaler:2.2.2 2.2.2   d8d6762 4.3 KiB
localhost:5000/stable/aerospike:0.2.1             0.2.1    4aff638 3.7 KiB
localhost:5000/stable/airflow:0.13.0              0.13.0   c46cc43 28.1 KiB
localhost:5000/stable/anchore-engine:0.10.0       0.10.0   3f3dcd7 34.3 KiB
```

Exporting a Chart from the Cache

If you wish to extract the source files of a chart once it is in the cache, it must first be exported to a local directory. Use the `helm chart export` command to export the chart:

```
$ helm chart export localhost:5000/myrepo/mychart:2.7.0
ref:     localhost:5000/myrepo/mychart:2.7.0
digest:  1b251d38cfe948dfc0a5745b7af5ca574ecb61e52aed10b19039db39af6e1617
size:    2.4 KiB
name:    mychart
version: 2.7.0
Exported chart to mychart/
```

The name of the chart will be used to determine the output path (e.g., `mychart/`).

Pushing a Chart to the Registry

Pushing (a.k.a. uploading) a chart to the registry allows for it to be used by others. Once you are already logged in to the registry and the chart you want to push has been saved to the cache, use the `helm chart push` command to push a chart:

```
$ helm chart push localhost:5000/myrepo/mychart:2.7.0
The push refers to repository [localhost:5000/myrepo/mychart]
ref:     localhost:5000/myrepo/mychart:2.7.0
digest:  1b251d38cfe948dfc0a5745b7af5ca574ecb61e52aed10b19039db39af6e1617
size:    2.4 KiB
name:    mychart
version: 2.7.0
2.7.0: pushed to remote (1 layer, 2.4 KiB total)
```

Pulling a Chart from the Registry

Once charts have been pushed to a registry, other users can then pull (a.k.a. download) them. Pulling charts from a registry places them into the local cache. To pull an existing chart from a registry, use the `helm chart pull` command:

```
$ helm chart pull localhost:5000/myrepo/mychart:2.7.0
2.7.0: Pulling from localhost:5000/myrepo/mychart
ref:     localhost:5000/myrepo/mychart:2.7.0
digest:  1b251d38cfe948dfc0a5745b7af5ca574ecb61e52aed10b19039db39af6e1617
size:    2.4 KiB
name:    mychart
version: 2.7.0
Status: Downloaded newer chart for localhost:5000/myrepo/mychart:2.7.0
```

Removing a Chart from the Cache

To remove a chart from the local cache, use the `helm chart remove` command:

```
$ helm chart remove localhost:5000/myrepo/mychart:2.7.0
2.7.0: removed
```

Related Projects

Helm's chart repository system has spawned a collection of open source tools to further enhance this experience. The following subsections cover some of the projects related to chart repositories.

ChartMuseum

Project homepage: https://github.com/helm/chartmuseum

ChartMuseum is a simple chart repository web server. Configure it to point to a storage location containing chart packages and it will dynamically generate *index.yaml*. It also exposes an HTTP API for uploading, querying, and deleting chart packages from storage. Additionally, it has a number of other configuration settings for auth, multitenancy, and caching that make it a popular choice for users hosting private or internal chart repositories.

ChartMuseum's Supported Backends

ChartMuseum supports a wide array of storage backends, including the following:

- Alibaba Cloud OSS Storage
- Amazon S3
- Baidu Cloud BOS Storage
- DigitalOcean Spaces
- etcd
- Google Cloud Storage
- Local filesystem
- Microsoft Azure Blob Storage
- Minio
- Netease Cloud NOS Storage
- Openstack Object Storage
- Oracle Cloud Infrastructure Object Storage
- Tencent Cloud Object Storage

Harbor

Project homepage: https://github.com/goharbor/harbor

Harbor is a full-featured registry with added security and management features. It provides a UI for Helm charts and leverages ChartMuseum on the backend as a multitenant chart respository. It also provides support for Helm's experimental OCI feature set.

Similar to Helm, *Harbor* is a graduated, top-level CNCF project.

Chart Releaser

Project homepage: https://github.com/helm/chart-releaser

Chart Releaser, or `cr`, is a command-line tool that leverages GitHub releases for hosting chart packages. It has the ability to detect charts in a Git repo, package them, and upload each of them as artifacts to GitHub releases named after the unique chart version.

Once charts have been uploaded using `cr`, the tool can also be used to generate an *index.yaml* file based on the contents of GitHub releases and associated artifacts. This repository index can then be hosted statically, on GitHub Pages or elsewhere.

S3 Plugin

Project homepage: https://github.com/hypnoglow/helm-s3

The S3 plugin is a Helm plugin that allows you to use a private Amazon S3 bucket as a chart repository.

GCS Plugin

Project homepage: https://github.com/hayorov/helm-gcs

The GCS plugin is a Helm plugin that allows you to use a private Google Cloud Storage bucket as a chart repository.

Git Plugin

Project homepage: https://github.com/aslafy-z/helm-git

The Git plugin is a Helm plugin that allows you to use a Git repository containing chart source files as a chart repository. It supports subpaths, custom references, and both HTTPS and SSH Git URLs.

## CHAPTER 8

Helm Plugins and Starters

As we've seen throughout this book, Helm has plenty of features and methods that aid in delivering applications on Kubernetes. However, it is also possible to customize and extend the functionality provided by Helm.

In this chapter we will discuss two ways to further enhance and customize your usage of Helm: *plugins* and *starters*.

Plugins allow you to add extra functionality to Helm and integrate seamlessly with the CLI, making them a popular choice for users with unique workflow requirements. There are a number of third-party plugins available online for common use cases, such as secrets management. In addition, plugins are incredibly easy to build on your own for unique, one-off tasks.

Starters expand the possibilities of using `helm create` to generate new Helm charts for different types of applications. For example, you might have a Helm chart built for an internal microservice that fits perfectly as an example for future microservices. You could convert the chart into a starter, which you can then use each time you begin a new project with similar requirements.

By leveraging plugins and starters, we can build on top of Helm's out-of-the-box functionality to simplify and automate everyday workflow tasks.

Plugins

Helm plugins are external tools that are accessible directly from the Helm CLI. They allow you to add custom subcommands to Helm without making any modifications to Helm's Go source code. This is similar in design to how plugin systems are implemented in other tools, such as `kubectl` (the Kubernetes CLI).

Additionaly, downloader plugins allow you to specify a custom protocol for communicating with chart repositories. This can be useful if you have some custom authentication method, or if you need to somehow modify the method in which Helm fetches charts from repositories

Installing Third-Party Plugins

Many third-party plugins are made open source and publicly available on GitHub. Many of these plugins use the "helm-plugin" tag/topic to make them easy to find. Refer to the documentation for Helm plugins on GitHub (*https://oreil.ly/3KwNb*).

Sample Publicly-Available Plugins

Here are just a few of the Helm plugins you can find on GitHub:

helm/helm-2to3
> Plugin for converting Helm 2 releases to Helm 3 releases in place

jkroepke/helm-secrets
> Plugin for effectively managing secrets in YAML format

maorfr/helm-backup
> Plugin to backup/restore Helm releases to/from a text file

karuppiah7890/helm-schema-gen
> Plugin to generate *values.schema.json* based on *values.yaml* (see Chapter 6 for more info on schematized values)

hickeyma/helm-mapkubeapis
> Plugin to update Helm release metadata that contains deprecated Kubernetes APIs

---

Once you have found a plugin to install, obtain its version control URL. This will be used as the means of obtaining the correct version of *plugin.yaml* and the rest of the plugin source code.

Git, SVN, Bazaar (Bzr), and Mercurial (Hg) URLs are currently supported. For Git, the version control URL looks something like `https://example.com/myorg/myrepo.git`.

For example, there is a simple plugin for managing Helm starters located in a git repo at *https://github.com/salesforce/helm-starter*. The version control URL for this plugin is `https://github.com/salesforce/helm-starter.git`.

To install this plugin, run `helm plugin install` passing the version control URL as the first argument:

```
$ helm plugin install https://github.com/salesforce/helm-starter.git
Installed plugin: starter
```

If the installation succeeds, you can proceed to use the plugin:

```
$ helm starter --help
Fetch, list, and delete helm starters from github.

Available Commands:
    helm starter fetch GITURL       Install a bare Helm starter from Github
                                    (e.g., git clone)
    helm starter list               List installed Helm starters
    helm starter delete NAME        Delete an installed Helm starter
    --help                          Display this text
```

To list all installed plugins, use the helm plugin list command:

```
$ helm plugin list
NAME     VERSION DESCRIPTION
starter 1.0.0   This plugin fetches, lists, and deletes helm starters from github.
```

To attempt to update the plugin, use the helm plugin update command:

```
$ helm plugin update starter
Updated plugin: starter
```

If you wish to the uninstall the plugin from your system, use the helm plugin remove command:

```
$ helm plugin remove starter
Uninstalled plugin: starter
```

Unless otherwise specified, Helm will use the *plugin.yaml* and source code located on the default branch of the Git repo when installing a plugin. If you wish to specify a Git tag to use, use the --version flag on install:

```
$ helm plugin install https://github.com/databus23/helm-diff.git --version v3.1.0
```

It is also possible to install plugins directly from a tarball URL. Helm will download the tarball and unpack it into the plugins directory:

```
$ helm plugin install https://example.com/archives/myplugin-0.6.0.tar.gz
```

In addition, you can install a plugin from a local directory:

```
$ helm plugin install /path/to/myplugin
```

Instead of copying the files, Helm will create symlinks to the original files:

```
$ ls -la "$(helm env HELM_PLUGINS)"
total 8
drwxrwxr-x 2 myuser myuser 4096 Jul  3 21:49 .
drwxrwxr-x 4 myuser myuser 4096 Jul  1 21:38 ..
lrwxrwxrwx 1 myuser myuser   21 Jul  3 21:49 myplugin -> /path/to/myplugin
```

This might be useful, for example, if you are actively developing a plugin. Making changes to *plugin.yaml* and other source files will be recognized immediately when invoking a symlinked plugin.

Custom Subcommands

Plugins have a number of useful features that enable seemless integration with the existing Helm user experience. Probably the most notable feature of Helm plugins is that each plugin supplies Helm with a custom, top-level subcommand. These subcommands even have the ability to leverage shell completion (covered later in this chapter).

A Bit of Helm Plugin History

One of the original features of Helm plugins was that they were provided with environment settings for connecting to Tiller, the deprecated Helm server-side component that existed in Helm 2. This was an important concept for plugin subcommands that needed to integrate closely with Helm, since anything involving Helm releases needed to route through Tiller.

In Helm 3, Tiller has been removed, and all communication to the Kubernetes API is performed by the Helm client itself. The plugin system, however, has remained.

Once a plugin is installed, a new command will become available for you to use based on the plugin's name. This new command integrates directly with Helm and will even show up in `helm help`.

For example, let's say we have a plugin installed called `inspect-templates` that gives us extra information about the YAML templates found within a chart. This plugin will provide you with an extra Helm command:

```
$ helm inspect-templates [args]
```

This will execute the `inspect-templates` plugin, passing along any arguments or flags provided to the underlying tool that the plugin executes upon invocation. The author of the plugin specifies some command that Helm should run as a subprocess each time the plugin is invoked (more info on how to specify this in "Building a Plugin" on page 155).

Plugins offer a happy alternative to augment Helm's existing feature set without the need to make any modifications to Helm itself.

Building a Plugin

Building a Helm plugin is a fairly straightforward process. Depending on the requirements and overall complexity of the plugin, it may require some programming knowledge; however, many plugins run just a basic shell command.

The underlying implementation

Consider the following Bash script, *inspect-templates.sh*, the underlying implementation for our example `inspect-templates` plugin:

```
#!/usr/bin/env bash
set -e

# First argument on the command line, a relative path to a chart directory
CHART_DIRECTORY="${1}"

# Fail if no chart directory provided or is invalid
if [[ "${CHART_DIRECTORY}" == "" ]]; then
    echo "Usage: helm inspect-templates <chart_directory>"
    exit 1
elif [[ ! -d "${CHART_DIRECTORY}" ]]; then
    echo "Invalid chart directory provided: ${CHART_DIRECTORY}"
    exit 1
fi

# Print a summary of the chart's templates
cd "${CHART_DIRECTORY}"
cd templates/
echo "----------------------"
echo "Chart template summary"
echo "----------------------"
echo ""
total="$(find . -type f -name '*.yaml' -maxdepth 1 | wc -l | tr -d '[:space:]')"
echo " Total number: ${total}"
echo ""
echo " List of templates:"
for filename in $(find . -type f -name '*.yaml' -maxdepth 1 | sed 's|^\./||'); do
    kind=$(cat "${filename}" | grep kind: | head -1 | awk '{print $2}')
    echo "  - ${filename} (${kind})"
done
echo ""
```

This script is what Helm will execute behind the scenes when a user runs `helm inspect-templates`.

 Underlying plugin implementations are not required to be written in Bash, Go, or any specific programming language. To the end-user of this plugin, it should appear to be just another part of the Helm CLI.

The plugin manifest

Each plugin is defined by a YAML file called *plugin.yaml*. This file contains plugin metadata and information regarding what command to run when the plugin is invoked.

Here's a basic example of *plugin.yaml* for the `inspect-templates` plugin:

```
name: inspect-templates ❶
version: 0.1.0 ❷
description: get a summary of a chart's templates ❸
command: "${HELM_PLUGIN_DIR}/inspect-templates.sh" ❹
```

❶ The name of the plugin.

❷ The version of the plugin.

❸ A basic description of the plugin.

❹ The command to run when this plugin is invoked.

Manual installation

First check the configured path for the plugin storage root directory:

```
$ HELM_PLUGINS="$(helm env HELM_PLUGINS)"
$ echo "${HELM_PLUGINS}"
/home/myuser/.local/share/helm/plugins
```

 Using a Custom Root Directory for Plugins

The root directory for plugins can be overridden by providing a custom path for the `HELM_PLUGINS` environment variable in the current environment.

Create a directory matching the name of the plugin (`inspect-templates`) inside the plugin storage root directory:

```
$ PLUGIN_ROOT="${HELM_PLUGINS}/inspect-templates"
$ mkdir -p "${PLUGIN_ROOT}"
```

Next, copy over *plugin.yaml* and *inspect-templates.sh* to the new directory, and make sure the script is executable:

```
$ cp plugin.yaml "${PLUGIN_ROOT}"
$ cp inspect-templates.sh "${PLUGIN_ROOT}"
$ chmod +x "${PLUGIN_ROOT}/inspect-templates.sh"
```

The end result

Here's what our `inspect-templates` plugin looks like in action:

```
$ helm inspect-templates
Usage: helm inspect-templates <chart_directory>
Error: plugin "inspect-templates" exited with error

$ helm inspect-templates nonexistant/
Invalid chart directory provided: nonexistant/
Error: plugin "inspect-templates" exited with error

$ helm create mychart
Creating mychart

$ helm inspect-templates mychart/
---------------------
Chart template summary
---------------------

 Total number: 5

 List of templates:
  - serviceaccount.yaml (ServiceAccount)
  - deployment.yaml (Deployment)
  - service.yaml (Service)
  - hpa.yaml (HorizontalPodAutoscaler)
  - ingress.yaml (Ingress)
```

Notice how the command-line arguments provided (i.e., `mychart/`) are passed directly to the script. This makes it easy for plugin authors to build standalone tools that accept any number of arguments or custom flags.

plugin.yaml

plugin.yaml is the name of the plugin manifest file that describes a plugin, its invocation command, and other important details.

Here is an example *plugin.yaml* that contains all possible options you can specify for your plugin:

```
name: myplugin ❶
version: 0.3.0 ❷
usage: "helm myplugin --help" ❸
description "a plugin that belongs to me" ❹
platformCommand: ❺
  - os: windows
    arch: amd64
    command: "bin/myplugin.exe"
command: "bin/myplugin" ❻
ignoreFlags: false ❼
hooks: ❽
```

```
    install: "scripts/install-hook.sh"
    update: "scripts/update-hook.sh"
    delete: "scripts/delete-hook.sh"
downloaders: ❾
  - command: "bin/myplugin-myp-downloader"
    protocols:
      - "myp"
      - "myps"
```

❶   The name of the plugin.

❷   The plugin version.

❸   The usage instructions for this plugin.

❹   A description of the plugin.

❺   Platform-specific commands. If a client matches an os/arch combo, run that command instead of the default one.

❻   Command to run when this plugin is invoked.

❼   Whether or not to supress Helm global flags passed (such as `--debug`) when passed as arguments to the plugin.

❽   Plugin hooks (see "Hooks" on page 159).

❾   Downloaders and associated protocols (see "Downloader Plugins" on page 160).

The `name` of the plugin will be the subcommand used to invoke this plugin from the Helm CLI (e.g., `helm myplugin`). Due to this, plugin names should not match any existing Helm subcommands (`install`, `repo`, etc.). The name can only contain the characters a–z, A–Z, 0–9, _, and -.

The plugin `version` should be a valid SemVer 2 version.

The `usage` and `description` for the plugin will be displayed when you run `helm help` and `helm help myplugin`. However, the plugin itself must handle its own flag parsing for things like `helm myplugin --help`.

The `command` is what Helm will execute in a subprocess when this plugin is invoked. If a section for `platformCommands` is defined, Helm will first check if the system matches the provided `os` (operating system) and `arch` (architecture), and if so, Helm will instead use the `command` defined in the matching entry. The `arch` field is optional, and if missing, just the `os` will be checked.

Here is the exact order in which Helm determines which command to run when a plugin is invoked, based on the contents of *plugin.yaml* and the runtime environment:

1. If `platformCommand` is present, it will be searched first.

2. If both `os` and `arch` match the current platform, search will stop and the platform-specific command will be executed.

3. If `os` matches and there is no more specific match, the platform-specific command will be executed.

4. If no `os`/`arch` match is found, the default top-level `command` will be executed.

5. Helm will exit with an error if no top-level `command` is present and no matches are found in `platformCommand`.

Hooks

Plugin hooks allow you to take additional actions when the plugin is installed, updated, or deleted.

For example, the underlying implementation for your plugin may be a platform-specific binary that must be downloaded from the internet. The URL for the binary varies depending on the user's operating system.

A script to handle this logic based on operating system might look something like the following:

```
#!/usr/bin/env bash

set -e

URL=""
EXTRACT_TO=""

if [[ "$(uname)" = "Darwin" ]]; then
    URL="https://example.com/releases/myplugin-mac"
    EXTRACT_TO="myplugin"
elif [[ "$(uname)" = "Linux" ]]; then
    URL="https://example.com/releases/myplugin-linux"
    EXTRACT_TO="myplugin"
else
    URL="https://example.com/releases/myplugin-windows"
    EXTRACT_TO="myplugin.exe"
fi

mkdir -p bin/
curl -sSL "${URL}" -o "bin/${EXTRACT_TO}"
```

By defining an install hook for our plugin, we can make it so that this script runs when a user installs this plugin.

To define a hook, add a hooks section to your *plugin.yaml*, defining commands for each event you want to respond to:

```
...
hooks:
  install: "scripts/install-hook.sh" ❶
  update: "scripts/update-hook.sh" ❷
  delete: "scripts/delete-hook.sh" ❸
```

❶ Command to run on helm plugin install

❷ Command to run on helm plugin update

❸ Command to run on helm plugin remove

Downloader Plugins

Some plugins have special functionality that allows them to be used as an alternative for downloading charts.

This is useful if you are storing charts in some way that is different than a pure chart repository, or if your chart repository implementation has extra requirements.

A *downloader plugin* defines one (or more) protocols that, if detected on the command line, will instruct Helm to download *index.yaml* or chart *.tgz* packages using the plugin versus Helm's internal download mechanism.

Here is an example of a *plugin.yaml* for a downloader plugin called "super-secure," which registers the ss:// protocol:

```
name: super-secure
version: 0.1.0
description: a super secure chart downloader
command: "${HELM_PLUGIN_DIR}/super-secure.sh"
downloaders:
  - command: "super-secure-downloader.sh" ❶
    protocols: ❷
      - "ss"
```

❶ Command to run when this plugin is invoked as a downloader

❷ Custom protocols declared by this plugin

Keep in mind that all plugins, including downloader plugins, define a custom top-level command (i.e., helm super-secure). The command for the plugin downloader can be identical to the command field; just beware that if you wish to use the plugin as both a standard plugin and as a downloader, it might become challenging to determine how it's being used. One way you could determine if the plugin is being used as a downloader is to check if the command is invoked with exactly four command-line arguments.

Downloader commands are always invoked with the following arguments:

```
<command> certFile keyFile caFile full-URL
```

The certFile, keyFile, and caFile arguments are derived from entries in a YAML configuration file, whose path is returned by $(helm env HELM_REPOSITORY_CONFIG), and are set when a repository is added using helm repo add (see Chapter 7 for more background). The full-URL argument is the full URL for the resource that is being downloaded, either an *index.yaml*, or chart *.tgz/.prov* file.

Let's check out the implementation for the ss:// protocol downloader defined by the super-secure plugin:

```
#!/usr/bin/env bash
set -e

# The fourth argument is the URL to the resource to download from the repo
URL="${4}"

# Replace "ss://" with "https://"
URL="$(echo ${URL} | sed 's/ss:/https:/')"

# Request the resource using the token, outputting contents to stdout
echo "Downloading $(basename ${URL}) using super-secure plugin..." 1>&2
curl -sL -H "Authorization: Bearer ${SUPER_SECURE_TOKEN}" "${URL}"
```

This downloader allows us to use a chart repository protected with token/bearer auth. It expects that the environment variable SUPER_SECURE_TOKEN is set, which will be used to formulate the header Authorization: Bearer <token> used when requesting a resource from a chart repository.

While the super-secure plugin is a great example of a simple downloader plugin, future versions of Helm may actually support bearer token auth out of the box.

Downloader plugins are expected to output the contents of the resource to stdout, so any extra logs etc. should be printed to stderr. This is why, in the line starting with echo, we redirect this message to stderr using 1>&2.

Once this plugin is installed, here's how we would add a chart repository protected by token auth:

```
$ export SUPER_SECURE_TOKEN="abc123"
$ helm repo add my-secure-repo ss://secure.example.com
Downloading index.yaml using super-secure plugin...
"my-secure-repo" has been added to your repositories
```

This repository URL will now show up in the local list of repositories, containing the ss:// protocol:

```
$ helm repo list
NAME            URL
my-secure-repo  ss://secure.example.com
```

Now the repository can be used just like any other repository, to download remote chart packages:

```
$ export SUPER_SECURE_TOKEN="abc123"
$ helm pull my-secure-repo/superapp
Downloading superapp-0.1.0.tgz using super-secure plugin...
$ ls
superapp-0.1.0.tgz
```

Downloader plugins provide a way for Helm users to extend the transfer mechanism for working with chart repositories by defining custom protocols. When Helm detects a custom protocol being used, it will attempt to locate an installed plugin that can handle it, then defers the resource request to that plugin.

Execution Environment

Since plugins are meant to extend Helm's functionality, they might need access to some of Helm's internal configuration files, or global flags provided on the command line.

To provide plugins access to this type of information, a series of known environment variables are provided to the plugin at runtime.

Here is a current list of all the environment variables available to plugins, in alphabetical order:

HELM_BIN
    The path to the Helm command being executed

HELM_DEBUG
    Value set for the global boolean --debug option ("true" or "false")

HELM_KUBECONTEXT
: Value set for the global `--kube-context <context>` option

HELM_NAMESPACE
: Value set for the global `--namespace <namespace>` option

HELM_PLUGIN_DIR
: Root directory of the current plugin

HELM_PLUGIN_NAME
: Name of the current plugin

HELM_PLUGINS
: Top-level directory containing all plugins

HELM_REGISTRY_CONFIG
: Root directory for registry configuration

HELM_REPOSITORY_CACHE
: Root directory for repository cache

HELM_REPOSITORY_CONFIG
: Root directory for repository configuration

Shell Completion

Helm has built-in support for shell autocompletion for both Bash and Z shell (Zsh) (see `helm completion --help`). This is helpful in situations where you cannot remember the name of a subcommand or flag you are attempting to use.

Plugins also have the ability to supply their own custom shell completions by using one of two methods: static autocompletion and dynamic completion.

Static autocompletion

By including a file called *completion.yaml* in the root of the plugin directory, Helm plugins can specify all of the expected flags and commands available for the plugin statically.

Here is an example *completion.yaml* for an imaginary zoo plugin:

```
name: zoo ❶
flags: ❷
  - disable-smells
  - disable-snacks
commands: ❸
  - name: price ❹
    flags:
      - kids-discount
```

```
      - name: animals
        commands:
          - name: list
            validArgs: ❺
              - birds
              - reptiles
              - cats
          - name: describe
            flags:
              - format-json
            validArgs:
              - birds
              - reptiles
              - cats
```

❶ The name of the plugin that this completion file is for

❷ A list of flags available (Note: these should not include a - or -- prefix)

❸ A list of subcommands available

❹ Name of an individual subcommand

❺ A list of valid options for the first parameter following a subcommand

Underneath the top-level `commands` section, another `commands` section can be speci-fied for nested subcommands (and recursively as many times as necessary). Each command in a `commands` section can contain its own list of `flags` and `validArgs`.

Helm's global flags, such as `--debug` or `--namespace`, are already handled by Helm's built-in shell completion, so it is not necessary to list these under `flags`.

If we begin trying to run the example `zoo` plugin, then press the Tab key, it should show us all of the available subcommands:

```
$ helm zoo  # (click tab)
animals  price
```

Now if we do the same, but add a `--disable-s` suffix prior to pressing the Tab key, we should see our flags:

```
$ helm zoo --disables-s  # (click tab)
--disable-smells  --disable-snacks
```

Using static completion, we are able to achieve parity with Helm's existing shell com-pletions, making plugins feel even more tightly integrated with the Helm user experience.

If you are in the process of developing a plugin, you must open a new terminal window for static shell completions to be refreshed.

Alternatively, you can run one of the following to get the latest completions in the current terminal:

```
source <(helm completion bash) # for Bash
source <(helm completion zsh)  # for Z shell
```

Dynamic completion

In some cases, the valid arguments for a given command may not be known ahead of time. For example, you may want to provide a list of Helm release names in your cluster as valid arguments for your plugin. This can be achieved using dynamic completion.

To enable dynamic completion, include an executable file named *plugin.complete* in the root of the plugin directory. This file can be any type of executable; for example, a shell script or binary.

For plugins containing a *plugin.complete* file, when completion is requested (i.e., pressing the Tab key), Helm will run this executable, passing along the text that needs completion as the first argument. This program should then return a list of possible results, each separated by a new line, and exit successfully (i.e., return code 0).

You might even decide to supply this completion functionality as part of the primary plugin program, using a simple wrapper script to trigger it using a flag such as --complete. Here is an example of a basic *plugin.complete* executable that does just this:

```
#!/usr/bin/env sh
$HELM_PLUGIN_DIR/my-plugin-program --complete "$@"
```

Building on the zoo plugin example, let's say the list of available animal categories is constantly changing and stored in a file called *animals.txt* in the user's home directory. Here's what *animals.txt* might look like:

```
birds
reptiles
cats
```

We want to be able to dynamically provide completion based on the contents of this file. Here is an example of a *plugin.complete* executable (Bash script) that could be used to provide dynamic completion:

```
#!/usr/bin/env bash
set -e
INPUT="${@}"
if [[ "${INPUT}" == "animals list"* ]]; then
    INPUT="$(echo "${INPUT}" | sed -e 's/^animals list //')"
    for flag in $(cat "${HOME}/animals.txt"); do
```

```
            if [[ "${flag}" == "${INPUT}"* ]]; then
                echo "${flag}"
            fi
        done
    fi
```

Now if we run the plugin and type in `animals list`, then press the Tab key, it should show us a list of all the available animal categories for listing:

```
$ helm zoo animals list  # (press Tab key)
birds     cats      reptiles
```

To ensure it's dynamic, let's add an extra category "monkeys" to *animals.txt* and try again:

```
$ echo "monkeys" >> "${HOME}/animals.txt"
$ helm zoo animals list  # (press Tab key)
birds     cats      monkeys    reptiles
```

It works!

This is just a simple example of using dynamic completion, but keep in mind that you could also query something remote, such as resources in your Kubernetes cluster, making this a powerful feature for plugins.

> If you are already using static completion using a *completion.yaml* file, then dynamic completion is not used, even if a `plugin.complete` executable is present in the plugin's root directory.

Starters

Starters, or starter packs, are similar to Helm charts, except that they are meant to be used as templates for new charts.

When you use the `helm create` command to create a new chart, this generates a new chart using Helm's built-in starter, which is a general-purpose chart using best practices.

To specify a custom starter, you can use the `--starter` option when creating a new chart:

```
$ helm create --starter basic-webapp superapp
```

Using starters allows us to leverage a chart that has been previously built for an application with a similar purpose. This is useful for bootstrapping new projects with similar requirements to be instantly ready to deploy to your Kubernetes environment.

Converting a Chart to a Starter

Any Helm chart can be converted into a starter. The only thing that separates a starter from a standard chart is the presence of dynamic references to the chart name in a starter's templates.

To convert a standard chart into a starter, replace any hardcoded references to the chart's name with the string <CHARTNAME>.

To demonstrate, let's take this simple ConfigMap template from a chart called *mychart*:

```
apiVersion: v1
kind: ConfigMap
metadata:
  name: {{ include "mychart.fullname" . }}
  labels:
    {{- include "mychart.labels" . | nindent 4 }}
data:
  hello: {{ .Values.hello | quote }}
```

Here's what that template would look like instead in a starter:

```
apiVersion: v1
kind: ConfigMap
metadata:
  name: {{ include "<CHARTNAME>.fullname" . }}
  labels:
    {{- include "<CHARTNAME>.labels" . | nindent 4 }}
data:
  hello: {{ .Values.hello | quote }}
```

 This chart must still contain a *Chart.yaml* file to work; however, it will be overwritten by the generator.

Making Starters Available to Helm

Before using a starter, you must first decide on a unique name for it, for example "basic-webapp" for a starter containing boilerplate templates for deploying a basic web application.

To make this starter a valid option to be used when the --starter flag is specified on the command line, it must exist as a directory under the filepath $(helm env HELM_DATA_HOME)/starters.

If this is the first starter you are adding, ensure that the top-level *starters* directory first exists:

```
$ export HELM_STARTERS="$(helm env HELM_DATA_HOME)/starters"
$ mkdir -p "${HELM_STARTERS}"
```

Then just copy the entire *basic-webapp* directory into that top-level directory:

```
cp -r basic-webapp "${HELM_STARTERS}"
```

Using Starters

Once a starter is available, you can generate new charts based on it by referencing its name on the command line:

```
$ helm create --starter basic-webapp superapp
Creating superapp
```

The structure of the newly generated chart will be identical to that of the starter. All references to <CHARTNAME> in the starter's templates will be replaced with the new chart's name (i.e., *superapp*).

Here's an example directory structure for a generated chart based on a starter that has only two templates defined, *deployment.yaml* and *service.yaml*:

```
$ tree superapp/
superapp/
├── Chart.yaml
├── templates
│   ├── _helpers.tpl
│   ├── deployment.yaml
│   └── service.yaml
└── values.yaml
```

From here, you could check this new chart into version control and start making changes to customize it for the given application.

Extending Helm Further

In this chapter, we have discussed how Helm can be extended using plugins and starters. However, there is one other way in which you can extend Helm: via open source contributions.

Everything in this book has been a reflection of thousands of open source contributions to the Helm project. While much of this work has been performed by maintainers (past and present), the majority of contributions have come from individuals around the world. This includes not only changes to the Go source code, but also testing and documentation updates.

Do you have something to contribute to the Helm project? Navigate to the Helm community landing page (*https://oreil.ly/9TloH*) to learn more!

Chart API Versions

This appendix covers the differences between chart API versions 2 and 1 (legacy).

The chart API version is specified in each chart's *Chart.yaml* file and is used by Helm to determine how to parse the chart and which feature sets are made available.

For new charts, API version 2 should generally be used. However, many publicly available charts were created prior to the genesis of API version 2, and use 1, the legacy API version. Here we will go into detail on each of these API versions and the ways in which they are different.

API Version 2

Chart API version 2 is the current API version that was introduced in Helm 3. This is the default API version used when new charts are created using `helm create`.

Charts using API version 2 are guaranteed to be supported by Helm 3, but not necessarily by Helm 2. If you are only planning to support Helm 3 and above, it is recommended to just use this API version.

The Chart.yaml File

The following is an example of a *Chart.yaml* file for a chart using API version 2:

```
apiVersion: v2 ❶
name: lemon
version: 1.2.3
type: application
description: When life gives you lemons, do the DevOps
appVersion: 2.0.0
home: https://example.com
icon: https://example.com/img/lemon.png
```

```
sources:
  - https://github.com/myorg/mychart
keywords:
  - fruit
  - citrus
maintainers:
  - name: Carly Jenkins
    email: carly@mail.cj.example.com
    url: https://cj.example.com
  - name: William James Spode
    email: william.j@mail.wjs.example.com
    url: https://wjs.example.com
deprecated: false
annotations:
  sour: 1
kubeVersion: ">=1.14.0"
dependencies:
  - name: redis
    version: ~10.5.7
    repository: https://kubernetes-charts.storage.example.com/
    condition: useCache,redis.enabled
  - name: postgresql
    version: 8.6.4
    repository: @myrepo
    tags:
      - database
      - backend
```

❶ Field denoting chart API version 2

Each of the top-level fields in this file will be described in detail in the following subsections.

Field: apiVersion

Required

The API version of this chart.

This field should *always* be set to v2.

Field: name

Required

The name of the chart.

In most cases, this should be 1-to-1 with the name of your application (i.e., lemon). If your application is broken into multiple, installable components, it is common to suffix this name with a description of the component; for example, lemon-frontend, lemon-backend, etc.

Chart names must be composed of lowercase letters, numbers, and dashes (-).

Field: version

Required

The current version of the chart, strictly formatted using Semantic Versioning 2.

Versioning Helm Charts

Semantic Versioning, if done correctly, can be extremely helpful. It lets the operator know what to expect during a software upgrade. You've likely already seen and used semantic versions. They are comprised of three numbers separated by a period (.), such as 3.1.2. Semantic versions follow the format MAJOR.MINOR.PATCH, where the following rules apply if each are incremented:

MAJOR

Indicates that breaking changes are made that are not backward compatible (e.g., 3.1.2 → 4.0.0)

MINOR

Indicates that there are newly available features that are backward compatible (e.g., 3.1.2 → 3.2.0)

PATCH

Indicates that one or more bugs were fixed, and that changes were made to make things work as originally expected without introducing any new features (e.g., 3.1.2 → 3.1.3)

Helm charts can be challenging to version properly because they are not typical software packages containing an application with features. As a rule of thumb, most updates to the chart version should be increments to the MINOR version.

For example, any time that you are adding new key-value pairs that are used inside templates, this can be considered a new "feature," since the options for configuration have been expanded. On the other hand, if you are modifying the way a certain value is used in a template, or removing a configuration setting entirely, this would be considered a breaking change, and you should increment the MAJOR version. Lastly, if you simply make a fix to a Helm chart that is not templating properly given an expected input, or is otherwise broken, this would be considered a bug fix and you should increment the PATCH version.

As for an initial version to use for your chart, choose 0.1.0 or 1.0.0. When the MAJOR version is 0 (e.g., 0.1.0), this technically indicates no promises will be made regarding breaking changes between MINOR and PATCH upgrades. Versions 1.0.0 and higher indicate a certain level of stability and a strict adherence to SemVer 2.

Field: type

Required

Specifies the chart type, which may be one on the following two types:

`application`
> A typical, installable chart

`library`
> A noninstallable chart containing common definitions, meant to be included as a dependency chart

This field is unique to API version 2. In API version 1, all charts are considered to be `application` charts. For more information on `library` charts, please see Chapter 6.

Field: description

A simple, one-sentence description of the chart.

Field: appVersion

The version of the application that the chart represents.

This field should match the version of the *software* you are deploying, not the chart itself. For example, if you're creating a new internal chart to deploy a custom configured Nginx 1.18.0, the `appVersion` field would be `1.18.0`, whereas the `version` field would be something more like `0.1.0` (initial version).

Field: home

An absolute URL to the homepage for the chart and/or application.

Field: icon

An absolute URL to an image that can be used as an icon for this chart.

This field is typically used by services such as Artifact Hub to display an appropriate image for the chart available for download.

Field: sources

One or more absolute URLs to the source code of the chart (if made available).

Field: keywords

A list of keywords or topics that the chart represents.

These are used by services such as Artifact Hub to group together charts by category or further enhance search capabilities.

Field: maintainers

A list of name/email/URL combinations for the person(s) who maintain the chart.

Field: deprecated

Whether or not the chart is deprecated.

This field is used by services such as Artifact Hub to determine when to remove chart listings.

Field: annotations

Additional mappings for the chart uninterpreted by Helm, made available for inspection by other applications.

Note: this field is *not* linked to Kubernetes annotations in any meaningful way; however, you may choose to define these as Kubernetes-specific annotations depending on how you decide to use this field.

Field: kubeVersion

A SemVer constraint specifying the minimum Kubernetes version required for the chart to properly install.

Some charts may use Kubernetes resource types and API groups that are only available on certain versions of Kubernetes. If an operator attempts to install a chart with an incompatible kubeVersion compared to that of the target cluster, an error will occur before any Kubernetes resources are provisioned.

Field: dependencies

A list of dependencies for the chart.

The chart dependencies listed here will be negotiated and placed appropriately into the *charts/* subdirectory when you run helm dependency update.

At a bare minimum, each entry under the dependencies block should contain a name subfield, and either a repository or an alias subfield. A repository should be an absolute URL to a valid chart repository (serving */index.yaml*). An alias should be the character "@" followed by the name of a previously added chart repository (e.g., @myrepo).

For more information about how to use chart dependencies, see "Chart Dependencies" on page 103.

The Chart.lock File

When a chart has dependencies listed under the `dependencies` field in *Chart.yaml*, a special file named *Chart.lock* is generated and updated each time you run the command `helm dependency update`. When a chart contains a *Chart.lock* file, operators can run `helm dependency build` to generate the *charts/* directory without the need to renegotiate dependencies.

Here is an example of a *Chart.lock* file generated based on the dependencies specified in the *Chart.yaml* example:

```
dependencies:
- name: redis
  repository: https://kubernetes-charts.storage.example.com/
  version: 10.5.7
- name: postgresql
  repository: https://charts.example.com/
  version: 8.6.4
digest: sha256:529608876e9f959460d0521eee3f3d7be67a298a4c9385049914f44bd75ac9a9
generated: "2020-07-17T11:10:34.023896-05:00"
```

Dynamic fields such as `conditions` and `tags` are stripped out, and this file simply contains the `repository`, `name`, and `version` that were resolved for each dependency during the update, as well as a `digest` (SHA-256) and a `generated` timestamp.

Notice that the `alias: "@myrepo"` setting for the PostgreSQL dependency has been converted into `repository: https://charts.example.com/`. This means that sometime prior to updating the dependencies, a chart repository was added using the following command:

```
$ helm repo add myrepo https://charts.example.com/
```

API Version 1 (legacy)

Chart API version 1 is the original API version, and the only version recognized by Helm 2. The `apiVersion` field in *Chart.yaml* was first introduced in Helm 3 and is not recognized by Helm 2. Using Helm 2, all charts are assumed to be adhering to API version 1. In Helm 3, the `apiVersion` is strictly required.

Charts using API version 1 are guaranteed to be supported by both Helm 2 and Helm 3, but may not be able to support certain features that will only be made available to Helm 3 in the future.

The Chart.yaml File

The format of the *Chart.yaml* file for charts using API version 1 is nearly identical to that of charts using API version 2, with a couple notable differences.

The following is an example of a *Chart.yaml* file for a chart using API version 1:

```
apiVersion: v1 ❶
name: lemon
version: 1.2.3
description: When life gives you lemons, do the DevOps
appVersion: 2.0.0
home: https://example.com
icon: https://example.com/img/lemon.png
sources:
  - https://github.com/myorg/mychart
keywords:
  - fruit
  - citrus
maintainers:
  - name: Carly Jenkins
    email: carly@mail.cj.example.com
    url: https://cj.example.com
  - name: William James Spode
    email: william.j@mail.wjs.example.com
    url: https://wjs.example.com
deprecated: false
annotations:
  sour: 1
kubeVersion: ">=1.14.0"
tillerVersion: ">=2.12.0"
engine: gotpl
```

❶ Field denoting chart API version 1

Differences from v2

As it compares to the *Chart.yaml* example for API version 2, there are some subtle differences:

- The `apiVersion` field is set to `v1` (Note: In Helm 2, this field is not strictly required).

- The `type` field is missing. There is no concept of library charts in API version 1.

- The `dependencies` field is missing. In API version 1, chart dependencies are specified in a dedicated file called *requirements.yaml* (as described later in this section).

- Two additional fields are present: `tillerVersion` and `engine`.

In many ways, the two chart API versions can essentially be considered Helm 2 charts (v1) versus Helm 3 charts (v2). This is especially true since chart API version 2 was introduced at the exact same time that Helm 3 was released.

The reason these versions aren't instead named v2 and v3 (denoting the Helm version) is because the API for charts is independently versioned from the API for the Helm CLI.

For example, if and when Helm 4 is released, it is possible that chart API version 2 will still be used. Likewise, if chart API version 2 is later determined to be insufficient for whatever reason, a new chart API version 3 could be introduced prior to another major Helm release.

Field: tillerVersion (legacy)

A SemVer constraint specifying the Tiller version required for the chart to properly install.

Tiller is a legacy Helm server-side component only used in Helm 2. This field is ignored entirely when using Helm 3.

Field: engine (legacy)

The name of the template engine to use. Defaults to *gotpl*.

The requirements.yaml File (Legacy)

In API version 1, there is an additional file called *requirements.yaml* that specifies the chart's dependencies. The format of this file is identical to the `dependencies` field as defined in API version 2.

Here is an example of a standalone *requirements.yaml* file:

```
dependencies:
  - name: redis
    version: ~10.5.7
    repository: https://kubernetes-charts.storage.example.com/
    condition: redis.enabled
  - name: postgresql
    version: 8.6.4
    repository: "@myrepo"
    tags:
      - database
      - backend
```

For a detailed description of each of the subfields, please see the subsection titled "Field: dependencies" under API version v2. In API version v2, the contents of this file are defined directly in *Chart.yaml*.

The requirements.lock File (Legacy)

In API version 1, the chart dependency lock file has the name *requirements.lock*. This file is identical in format and purpose to the *Chart.lock* file described under API version 2, just with a different name. For more information, please see the subsection titled "The Chart.lock File" under API version 2.

Chart Repository API

In Chapter 7, we covered chart repositories. This appendix briefly covers the chart repository API, the underlying specification that enables Helm to work with chart repositories.

The chart repository API is lightweight because there is only one required HTTP endpoint that must be implemented: GET /index.yaml.

In 99% of cases, chart repositories also serve chart package tarballs (*.tgz*) and any associated provenance files (*.prov*). However, it is also possible to host these files on a separate domain.

As described in detail in Chapter 7, *index.yaml* represents the repository index, containing a complete list of all the available chart versions in the repository. The format of this file is specific to Helm, and it currently has only one API version (1).

index.yaml

When implementing the chart repository API, your service must provide an HTTP GET /index.yaml route relative to the repository URL provided. The response from this request must return a status code 200 OK, and the response body must be a valid *index.yaml* as described in the following.

The GET /index.yaml endpoint does not need to be at the root of the URL path. For instance, given a provided repository URL such as *https://example.com/charts*, the GET /index.yaml route must be accessible at *https://example.com/charts/index.yaml*.

The index.yaml Format

Following is a simple, valid *index.yaml* with a single chart version (`superapp-0.1.0`):

```
apiVersion: v1 ❶
entries: ❷
  superapp:
  - apiVersion: v2
    appVersion: 1.16.0
    created: "2020-04-28T10:12:22.507943-05:00" ❸
    description: A Helm chart for Kubernetes
    digest: 46f9ddeca12ec0bc257a702dac7d069af018aed2a87314d86b230454ac033672 ❹
    name: superapp
    type: application
    urls: ❺
    - superapp-0.1.0.tgz
    version: 0.1.0
generated: "2020-04-28T11:34:26.779758-05:00" ❻
```

❶   The repository API version (must always be `v1`).

❷   A map of unique chart names in the repository to a list of all available versions.

❸   The timestamp of when the tarball was created using `helm package`.

❹   A SHA-256 digest of the tarball.

❺   A list of URLs where the chart can be downloaded. These URLs can be absolute, and even hosted on separate domain(s). If a relative path is provided, it is considered relative to *index.yaml*. Usually only one URL entry is provided per chart version, but multiple can be provided, and Helm will try to download the next item in the list if the previous one is inaccessible.

❻   The timestamp of when this *index.yaml* file was generated, in RFC 3339 format.

With the exception of the fields `created`, `digest`, and `urls`, all of the fields on each individual chart version are defined by the chart API (`name`, `version`, etc.). Please see Appendix A for more info.

When Is index.yaml Downloaded?

There are five noteworthy scenarios when Helm downloads or redownloads the repository index:

1. When initially adding a chart repository:

   ```
   $ helm repo add myrepo https://charts.example.com
   ```

2. When updating all chart repositories:

```
$ helm repo update
```

3. When updating dependencies (disabled with the `--skip-refresh` flag):

```
$ helm dependency update
```

4. When building dependencies from a lock file (disabled with the `--skip-refresh` flag):

```
$ helm dependency build
```

5. When installing a local chart with dependencies using the `--dependency-update` flag:

```
$ helm install myapp . --dependency-update
```

When Is the Cached Version of index.yaml Used?

Once *index.yaml* is downloaded, it is stored in a local cache and used whenever you reference the unique name you have associated with the repository (e.g., "myrepo").

There are five noteworthy scenarios when Helm makes use of the locally cached repository index:

1. When pulling a chart from a repo:

```
helm pull myrepo/mychart
```

2. When installing a chart from a repo:

```
helm install myapp myrepo/mychart
```

3. When upgrading a release based on a chart from a repo:

```
helm upgrade myapp myrepo/mychart
```

4. When searching for charts to use:

```
helm search repo myrepo/
```

5. When updating dependencies using the `--skip-refresh` flag (and a dependency contains an `alias` subfield such as `"@myrepo"`):

```
helm dependency update --skip-refresh
```

.tgz Files

.tgz files in a repository represent individual chart versions, packaged as compressed tarballs.

There is no requirement for the URL path for these files as they are hosted in the repository; however, they must be able to be downloaded when they are requested by Helm. The status code of the response must be a `200 OK`, and the response body should be the content of the *.tgz* in binary form.

When Are .tgz Files Downloaded?

There are three noteworthy scenarios when Helm downloads chart package *.tgz* files:

1. When pulling a chart from a repo:

   ```
   helm pull myrepo/mychart
   ```

2. When installing a chart from a repo:

   ```
   helm install myapp myrepo/mychart
   ```

3. When upgrading a release based on a chart from a repo:

   ```
   helm upgrade myapp myrepo/mychart
   ```

.prov Files

.prov files in a repository represent chart version signature files, signed with GNU Privacy Guard. These files are *optional* and are used for verification purposes.

Unlike *.tgz* files, *.prov* files have a unique URL path requirement. They must be accessible at the path of the associated *.tgz* suffixed with *.prov*. For example, if a *.tgz* file is located at *https://charts.example.com/superapp-0.1.0.tgz*, then the *.prov* file must be located at *https://charts.example.com/superapp-0.1.0.tgz.prov*.

The status code of the response must be a 200 OK, and the response body should be the content of the *.prov* in binary form.

When Are .prov Files Downloaded?

There are three noteworthy scenarios when Helm downloads chart signature *.prov* files:

1. When pulling a chart from a repo with the --verify flag:

   ```
   helm pull myrepo/mychart --verify
   ```

2. When installing a chart from a repo with the --verify flag:

   ```
   helm install myapp myrepo/mychart --verify
   ```

3. When upgrading a release based on a chart from a repo with the --verify flag:

   ```
   helm upgrade myapp myrepo/mychart --verify
   ```

Index

About the Authors

Matt Butcher is a cofounder/creator of the Helm project. He leads a team of open source engineers at Microsoft Azure. Matt is also the cocreator of *The Illustrated Children's Guide to Kubernetes* (with Karen Chu, Cloud Native Computing Foundation) and has authored eight other books (two with Matt Farina). He holds a Ph.D. in philosophy. When not coding, he enjoys drinking great coffee or hiking in the Colorado Rockies.

Matt Farina is a maintainer on the Helm project and has been contributing to open source projects for more than 15 years. He cofounded and cochairs the Kubernetes Apps Special Interest Group (SIG), which focuses on running workloads on Kubernetes. Matt works as a software architect at SUSE where he works on Kubernetes and developer tooling. He has previously authored two books alongside Matt Butcher. Creative problem solving and helping people are two driving forces for Matt's work with software.

Josh Dolitsky is a maintainer of the Helm project and founder of the *ChartMuseum* project. He is the owner and lead engineer of Blood Orange, a software consulting firm specialized in helping with DevOps, CI/CD, and Kubernetes. Josh has a penchant for undertaking ambitious software projects and seeing them to completion (for the most part). He is a chronic user of airplane mode while not on an aircraft, and relishes the many nondigital joys in life.

Colophon

The animal on the cover of *Learning Helm* is a little grebe (*Tachybaptus ruficollis*), also known as a dabchick, a small water bird found in a large range extending across Europe, Africa, and southern Asia.

The little grebe has a pointed bill, which darkens from yellow to black as it matures, surrounded by white accents. Its mostly dark plumage, which runs down the bird's back to its blunt rear, is offset by a rust-colored neck and a lighter abdomen. The little grebe's breeding call is a trilled *weet-weet-weet* that has been likened to a horse's whinny.

Its legs are set far back, like all grebes, and while it has difficulty walking on land the dabchick is a talented swimmer and diver. Thus, it prefers to dine on insects, mollusks, tadpoles, and small fish and build its nest at the water's edge. Little grebe chicks are fed feathers by their parents to create a soft stomach lining that prevents damage from fish bones and shells.

While the little grebe's conservation status is currently listed as of Least Concern, many of the animals on O'Reilly covers are endangered; all of them are important to the world.

The cover illustration is by Karen Montgomery, based on a black and white engraving from *Elements of Ornithology*. The cover fonts are Gilroy Semibold and Guardian Sans. The text font is Adobe Minion Pro; the heading font is Adobe Myriad Condensed; and the code font is Dalton Maag's Ubuntu Mono.

O'REILLY®

There's much more where this came from.

Experience books, videos, live online training courses, and more from O'Reilly and our 200+ partners—all in one place.

Learn more at oreilly.com/online-learning

Milton Keynes UK
Ingram Content Group UK Ltd.
UKHW021938260324
440133UK00006B/20